Going Beyond

$2

Going Beyond

Building Your Life in Difficult Times

Philip Mondragon

iUniverse, Inc.
New York   Bloomington

Going Beyond
Building your life in difficult times

iUniverse books may be ordered through booksellers or by contacting:

iUniverse
1663 Liberty Drive
Bloomington, IN 47403
www.iuniverse.com
1-800-Authors (1-800-288-4677)

ISBN: 978-0-595-53051-9 (pbk)
ISBN: 978-0-595-63105-6 (ebk)

Printed in the United States of America

iUniverse rev. date: 4/20/2009

For my mother, Hazel Hawkinson
Thomas Lucius Berkley and Velda
Barack Obama and his generation

Maruja and the thread of love,
the way out of the labyrinth

Contents

Acknowledgments

I am grateful to many good people who helped me produce this book and the experiences described in it. They include:

Dr. J. Harold Ennis for prophetic vision. Winifred Van Etten for teaching. Dr. Vivian Antaki and Tim Havard for writing tips. Seth Segal for a worldview. Dr. Bernard Lafayette for his loyalty to Dr. King and to all of us. Norie Sekimoto for her patient example. Enrique Giraud and Fuji for photo technology. Andres Flores for leadership, and Ernesto Flores for his humanity.

Amundsen editor Barbara Thiele Beese and Bob Fosse who gave us an example of how to develop potential. Stosh and Peggy Christopoulos for always being there in Chicago. Pete Pantos and Bill Friberg for their kindness. Spike Spear and Jerry Stubig for their sacrifices. John Greenhill and Taylor Belcher III for professionalism.

I thank repeatedly my loving wife, Maruja, my supportive children Luis, Chema, and Anamary, and my grandchildren, including Marius and Wojtek, who motivated me to share life and its consequences across generations.

PREFACE

I was high on a yellow tower balcony looking down into Santa Lucia Bay in Acapulco, and I watched sunlight flow on blue waves washing into a fine-grained sandy shore. I found myself imagining how to tell this story.

I remembered the old Chicago writer who saw life as a loose-flowing thing and said that fragments of experience can be pieced together to tell a story that is complete and has its own beauty. I thought of the Picasso sketches at the Reina Sofia Museum in Madrid and how he wove them together to paint *Guernica*. The fragments of my story were about a search for the self among countries and cultures, through experience, and by looking inward. My story was filled with rivers and labyrinths, illusions and realities, and defeats and a few victories.

When I was younger I saw life in orderly black-and-white lines. Seeing below me an arched cluster of green palm trees floating in shimmering waves of heat, weaving in the air like Masai warriors shaking luxurious headdresses, I was reminded that life is multicolored, contradictory, and elusive—far beyond our attempts to force it into rigid patterns.

In the beginning I found simplicity on the plains of Illinois. Challenge during infantry training in Kansas. Complexity while working as an intelligence agent in Japan and its outlying islands. Patience and reward in learning to adjust to the subtle ways of Mexico. Fulfillment in the multicultural history and dignity of Spain.

During my journey I traveled across three rivers: the Mississippi, the Bravo, and the Guadalquivir. I transcended from blindness to seeing, to feeling, and finally to understanding. I found a rich and addictive wine in intelligence work. I was trained to find the truth. I did this, and along the way I found love for the people I dealt with and learned to understand.

I know now that life is indeed a loose-flowing thing. We make only a few key decisions in our lives, and they determine who we become. They bring unexpected consequences that we can understand best when we are willing to examine them across generations.

Winter

I miss the golden leaves of fall
And my African older brother
Thomas Lucius Berkley
He was a Man
As men ought to be
And seldom are
I do not miss the pain of life
Replaced in time
With humility and patience and love
And a semblance of wisdom
Across generations
And cultures
From the song of the zentzontle*
And the color of jade
And the enervating perfume of flowers
To Oshima* and tradition
And the land of Rashomon*
To La Dama de Elche*
And endless migrations
Across time and space
The Arabs and Jews of Spain
The towers and tears of Granada
Orange blossoms and scents
Andalusia
Tauromaquia*
Jerez de la Frontera

The soul and pride of the South
Unamuno from the North
Demanding immortality
Erroneous focus on the self
Resting in the dreams and madness
Of Don Quixote
And now
The virtual world
Of bits and bytes and quantifications
Secularizations and polarizations
Of populations and civilizations
Science and the coming anarchy
Asgard* and the runes of knowledge
The Ice Giant comes tomorrow
Who will be here to face him?

* zentzontle: Aztec songbird
* Oshima: Japanese island
* Rashomon: Japanese folk tale
* Dama de Elche: Spanish statue
* Tauromaquia: Spanish bullfighting
* Asgard: Scandinavian heaven

Alone

He was a child, and during the day he lived alone and frightened. His father had abandoned him on a winter day in Chicago during the Depression, and after that his mother began to work in a factory in Ravenswood in order to feed him. He did not know why his father had left, but he concluded that it was his fault and that he had done something terribly wrong although he did not know what it was. The anxiety and pain that grew inside him began to express itself in a facial tic that he could not control. It distracted him and often left him unable to think.

He had only one escape during the day. His mother had taught him to read, and by the time he entered primary school he had already begun his friendship with books. Books were his inner world. They paid no attention to his shyness and trauma. They were fair and they helped him. He loved books.

In primary school he read every book in his classroom. After that the teacher let him leave class and go to the library to browse and read whatever interested him. The library became his home. In its books he traveled and met people and learned how they lived and did things in ways different from the ways of Chicago.

In the evenings his mother came home, and the hurt would stop most of the time. She was a gentle lady, and the child could always be certain of her love. She sewed used clothing for him to wear, she cooked food for him, and she let him read to her. He read whatever he found in his books that he thought would make her happy. He knew that she suffered and so he decided he would never tell her about his hurt. It stayed locked inside him and made him wonder why people treated him nicely when he knew they did not love him and he did not deserve their kindness.

STARTING OUT

Starting out in Chicago

MEMORABLE WOMAN

Hazel Hawkinson, a memorable woman and mother

Snow Angels

Winter in Chicago
Depression times
Cold white snow
Covered with yellow light
From aging lampposts
And soot from passing trains
You wore the cut-down clothing
Of older people
And their oversized shoes
Stuffed with pairs of stockings
So you could walk in them
Across the snow-covered streets
And take food
To your stepfather
Who drove a bus
And then shoveled rock salt
On the icy night streets of Chicago
He had his job
And you had yours
And that was how the family
Worked and survived
And one evening

Coming back from the bus depot
Crossing an empty piece of land
Sooty and yellow and white
In the night
You laid down in the snow
Eyes to the sky
Snow melting into your neck
And carefully moved
Your arms and legs
In wide repeated arcs
Creating the form
Of a clean and perfect snow angel
And when you stood up
Without disturbing the snow
And saw what you had done
You knew
That whatever happened
Tomorrow and later in life
You could always make snow angels
In your heart
And you were grateful
Because you understood

Coal

The boy was eleven, and it was four o'clock in the morning. In the cold predawn he clung to the top of a mountain of snow-covered coal in the yards next to the Chicago Northwestern railway tracks. He lay there frozen by the cold and by his fear that the watchman on the other side of the pile would hear him, circle around carrying his lantern, and see him lying there in the dark. He was frightened and ashamed and puzzled. Why had he come here to steal coal?

It was an unusually cold winter in Chicago, and there had been a family meeting to decide how to survive it. They were poor. They had no money to heat their flat in the woodframe building on Ravenswood. His stepfather was a Depression-times bus driver, a refined man whose family had emigrated from Alsace-Lorraine. He said, "We are a good family, and we are honest. But if we cannot buy coal to heat our house, we will freeze. We have no money for anything except food."

"I need to buy gloves so I can deliver newspapers," the boy's stepbrother interjected, showing his hands, which were bluish red from the icy air outside.

"I already drive an eight-hour shift, and then I shovel rock salt and sand from a truck," his stepfather replied. "And still there isn't enough money for us to survive."

It was as simple as that. The boy knew it was true. Every afternoon he stood in the bus depot at the dispatcher window selling dime magazines to tired drivers who were turning in the fare money they had collected during their trips downtown into the Loop.

His stepfather made the decision, and that night the boys went to bed early. They left the house in the darkness before morning, each carrying a large burlap sack. They crossed Ravenswood and climbed the barbed-wire fence and then the high mound of dirt and stone that served as a bed for the railroad tracks. It was only a few more steps to the coal piles, and in the dark he did not see anyone. He climbed cautiously to the top of the nearest mound and began to shovel pieces of coal by hand into his burlap sack.

Now he lay flattened against the coal pile, frozen by the sound of the approaching guard. He did not know what would happen. He only wondered why his family was forced to steal in order to survive. It would take years for him to piece together the truth of the times in which he was living. To get over the shame. To understand the experience and the lessons in it.

Fishing in the North

When things got better, the boy's stepfather bought an old Ford Flivver, and sometimes on weekends they would drive north with his uncles to Fox Lake and Pistakee and Nippersink to fish for bluegills and bass and pickerel. The trips began before dawn. The tired men sat silently in the car as it chugged slowly along the rutted roads of northern Illinois. Philip did not dare interrupt their silence. Instead he watched the darkened towns pass by. Sometimes the men would stop at a roadside café in one of the towns to eat crisp strips of bacon and eggs fried in bacon grease.

When they reached their destination, they would rent an old wooden boat for one dollar, and the boy would row for them out into the lake. He liked to row, and besides he was not as tired as the men. When the boat reached a location that the men approved, Philip would drop the cement-can anchor, bait the poles, and set them out. The men would watch with him until one by one they fell asleep. Rest and sleep were the real reasons for most of the fishing trips.

One morning at Fox Lake they decided to rent a better boat from a German who ran a boat-and-bait service next to his tavern, which blared polkas from a jukebox at all hours of the day and night. The man received them but refused to rent to them. He pointed to a sign that read, "For Gentiles Only."

Philip was puzzled. He did not know what a Gentile was. Years later a Swiss banker would inform him that the name of his stepfather's highly Catholic family was in fact Jewish by origin. Somewhere in history they had lived their own Diaspora. But Philip, who had a different last name from his stepfather, did not understand why the tired men could not rent a rowboat.

As he grew, Philip never accepted the ridiculous logic that people were to be divided into groups and punished because of their names or physical traits. Jews, Germans, African Americans, Irish Catholics, and others became his friends and teachers. They taught him lessons he never could have learned alone.

My Chicago

Working on Wabash
The South Side
Near Colosimo's
Torrio and Capone
The West was Cicero
Oak Park and Hemingway
Untouched
The North Side O'Banion
And Touhy and Moran
The Biograph
And Dillinger's last movie
The Clark Street car passing
The Saint Valentine's Day garage
On Easter morning
On your way to the county jail
To sing hymns
To the prisoners
Your school is filled
With the children of immigrants
Fosse will dance his way to fame
Stubig will become a detective
And die from a shotgun blast
While his classmate
Works as a hit man
For the Mafia
Timko will go to jail
Along with the Swede

The Greek will die in Korea
And in the construction gang
The Italian workers
Believe a gun
Is a sign of rising status
When you go to the tavern
On payday to cash your check
In the room behind the bar
Filled with gamblers and skimmers
The cop smiles
And opens the door
This is your town
In your time
And you love Chicago
Raw and powerful
Proud of what it is
And what it will become
It will always be yours
Again and again
Putting your feet on the ground
Helping you find reality
Behind the smoke and mirrors
Of self-righteousness
And predictable human behavior

Doors

He was seventeen, and he did not intend to study at a university. He had never been inside one and had never talked to a university graduate. He worked part-time after school at a street construction site on Wilson Avenue in Chicago, breaking concrete with a jackhammer. He was already earning more money than his stepfather, who drove a CTA bus downtown every day into the Loop and then back to the North Side for a twenty minute break only to repeat the process again and again.

One day a teacher from school called him to her office. "I have seen your test scores. They are far above average. You could win a scholarship and earn a university education."

"Why should I? It isn't my world."

"You might be surprised. The experience could open a new world to you."

He thought about it for days. Was it worth looking into? He had only average grades and a nervous facial tic. And though he doubted his personal worth, he had never stopped reading since childhood. He still read every book in the schoolroom, and his teachers still let him leave classes and go to the school library to read whatever attracted him.

He decided to take the scholarship test, but he did not study for it. He was not convinced that a college degree had much practical value. On the Friday evening before the test, he went to a movie with the girl he was dating. The following morning he rode his stepfather's bus downtown to the LaSalle Street office of the scholarship fund. During the exam he sat surrounded by well-dressed, self-assured young men. He realized that he was from an entirely different world.

He was surprised when he won one of the scholarships that covered his tuition. His teacher helped him find a Midwestern liberal arts college that would let him work as a waiter and dishwasher to pay for his room and board. He had to cover every expense himself. His family was progressing, but there was no extra money for him.

Early in September he traveled across the Mississippi River by bus into Iowa and reached the college campus. He could not sleep that night. He kept asking himself why he was at the college and not where he belonged, among the workers in his construction gang in Chicago.

Premise

Midwestern prairie simplicity
Common sense and clarity
In the street
Close to the people
And their roots
Close to the ground

While selfish climbers
Rise in higher circles
Building their interests
Widening the gaps
Ignoring the plateaus
Of honest reflection

Choose a better premise
And live by it
Lincoln did
Understood envy
Accepted ridicule
Held his ground

Lincoln
Gandhi
Martin Luther King
Stood with the people
Helped them find the truth
Showed them how to live

Find your premise
Live by it
Build a life
That is real
Grateful for the opportunity
To become yourself

Crossing the Rio Bravo

By the time he completed his studies at the private Midwestern college, war had broken out in Korea. He volunteered for the U.S. Army Counterintelligence Service. Before he left for training at Fort Riley in Kansas and Fort Holabird near Baltimore, his mother gave him an airplane ticket and the address of his father in Mexico City. She wanted him to know his father.

He had never met a Mexican. He spoke textbook Spanish and could not pronounce his own family name. His cultural knowledge covered only the Anglo-Saxon north. His mother was Scandinavian, and his father was a hot-blooded blonde criollo from Mexico City. Philip carried the north-south contrast inside him and did not know it.

On a winter morning in Chicago he boarded an American Airlines flight to Mexico City without knowing where he would sleep that evening. The businessman seated next to him on the plane suggested the Hotel Roosevelt, as it was clean and not very expensive. Philip registered at the hotel and slept nervously, and the next morning he took a green-and-white taxi to the offices of Pemex, the national petroleum company on Avenida Juarez across the street from the Hotel Regis. He knew that his father worked at Pemex.

The secretary who received him told him that his father was the Export Director for the Mexican petroleum industry that President Cardenas had nationalized in 1938. Aided by a brilliant mind and an impending World War II, his father had developed a successful international export sales program using the Pemex office in New York as his base. He had lived New York City for much of the time Philip had spent trying to find his way in Chicago.

His father was clearly surprised by the visit and invited him to lunch and then to his elegant home in suburban Lomas Chapultepec. He went there and found that he had a half brother and two half sisters. The family was cordial and asked him why he did not stay in Mexico instead of joining the army in wartime. Philip replied that he could not abandon the country that had raised him and given him a university education.

He stayed in Mexico for seven days at the Hotel Roosevelt, refusing an invitation to sleep at his father's house, though he did visit with his

15

father's family and got to know the warmth of Mexican culture. When he returned to Chicago he realized that his mother had purposely introduced him to a new world. He decided he would explore it after completing his counterintelligence work, which would take him to the Far East.

Sergeant Brown

Philip trained first with the infantry at Fort Riley in Kansas, where he learned to be a platoon leader. He felt confident once he found that he enjoyed the challenges of responsibility, discipline, long marches, cold meals in the rain, and the austere life in the military. His friends were surprised at the ways he tried to face and solve each situation.

One morning another trainee advised him, "Watch out for Sergeant Brown. He is a war hero—won the Silver Star in combat. Came back wounded. He is our best cadre man, and he demands a lot from his people."

Philip filed the warning away in his mind, and three days later he was inspecting a barracks building when a round-faced, seventeen-year-old boy walked in to interrupt him.

"Who are you?" Philip asked impatiently.

"I'm Sergeant Brown" the boy replied.

Philip saw in a moment that he was face to face with something real. The boy based himself on character, not age. Philip understood this and gave him immediate respect.

From that day on Philip did not pay much attention to age. He focused instead on the actions and accomplishments of the people around him. Some were spoiled children at twenty. Others were men at seventeen.

The lesson served him time and again later in life when he refused to evaluate people simply by their age and instead recognized their underlying skills. He never had a problem working with younger people he respected, and together they built successful projects in business, social service, and family.

The Mexican

Infantry training at Fort Riley gave Philip the opportunity to test his ideas and observations against reality. When he accepted reality instead of hiding from it by lying to himself, he found he became a stronger and better person.

The talkers were the easiest ones to identify. If he listened to them and believed what they said, they became invincible men of unlimited talent who could do anything. One such trainee was an athletic, semi-professional baseball player whose background and physical conditioning made his first weeks of training an easy experience for him. By the third week, however, he began to falter. His tired muscles pained him, and on long marches he walked slow and lagged behind the platoon. One predawn morning when the whistle sounded for immediate assembly, he refused to get out of bed. It took two cadre men to lift his upper bunk mattress and roll him onto the floor, his face reflecting surprise and shock at the way he was treated.

In the beginning of training, the biggest man in the group served as platoon leader. He snarled at smaller people around him and demanded more than he gave. One day when the men were to receive their pre-overseas vaccines, he led them to the open door of a barracks building where the medics inside stood next to sets of doors and held menacing needles. The big man looked at the needles and fainted. That was the end of leadership by physical type.

The best soldier in the platoon was a short, wiry Mexican named Anselmo Montez. He did not have an ounce of fat on his body, and at the end of a twenty-mile march he carried at least two rifles for the bigger men around him so that they might finish. He always did this with a smile.

COUNTERINTELLIGENCE

Field agent at Army Counterintelligence headquarters on Okinawa

Okinawa

After Philip completed infantry training he was transferred to the counterintelligence center at Fort Holabird, which was near Baltimore. He trained in this esoteric specialty and then was shipped to the island of Okinawa, where he worked from a station north of Naha City. His initial assignments were designed to show the U.S. Army its own counterintelligence weaknesses. When he began to work as an agent in the field, he was amazed at what he found.

In one case his team was assigned to carry out a midnight evaluation of security at the Ryukyu Regional Command Headquarters, located ten minutes from his base. The team easily penetrated the darkened headquarters building, and Philip found himself in front of a huge floor-to-ceiling wall safe with doors like those on bank vaults back in the United States.

He examined the doors and wondered how he might open them. It occurred to him that people with poor memories often jotted down key information. He sat down in the chair of the G-2 officer responsible for the safe and its contents, turned over a large desk blotter, and found the safe's combination written clearly on the reverse side. He called over a team specialist, and it took only a moment for the man to dial the combination and open the lock. Philip swung the huge doors open and began to examine documents containing the Army's top regional secrets. The exercise taught him that the weakest link in technology was the human mind. He never forgot that.

On another occasion, Philip's team was assigned to infiltrate the U.S. Navy invasion landing exercise at Buckner Bay, which was on the eastern coast of Okinawa near Shuri Castle. The exercise involved multiple ships gathered offshore and was directed by an admiral from a command center located atop a high knoll with a full view of all ocean vessels and the troops coming ashore. In spite of the naval personnel assigned to protect the admiral and his command center, Philip was able to sever communication wires, talk his way past naval security personnel, and stand directly behind the admiral's chair, where he could hear and see the entire operation.

Philip never understood why people did not take security threats seriously. They usually thought that training should be different from life, but they were wrong. The closer one is to reality, even in practice, the better one's probability of surviving and winning in any situation.

Japanese Islands

Philip enjoyed his counterintelligence work on the island of Okinawa. His CIC office had a CIA base hidden directly behind it. Observers never noticed the cars passing quietly through the first location to reach the second.

He found that he was highly suited for counterintelligence work and the collection of positive intelligence. When his superiors offered to teach him local names and interests, he asked to be left alone for two days in the file room, where he used his reading experience and a now almost-photographic memory to brief himself in depth about factual detail. He became the leading agent in his group, and older agents coached him as he established and operated an intelligence net that included the president of the Ryukyu Island chain and leaders of the major political parties. It was the first of many nets that he would organize and operate later in life.

One year out of college and he was meeting regularly with the president of the island chain in order to identify political trends and threats in the area. The president, a former schoolteacher, was pro-U.S. and always wanted to provide rosy data. The Socialist leader was more independent, and the Communist Peoples Party head was militant and fortunately quite direct. By meshing these sources with other key people at lower echelons and in diverse fields, Philip usually produced reports that were accurate and hopefully useful to his country. He did not yet know that intelligence, when it rises in the recipient chain, is sometimes distorted in order to tell high-echelon political leaders what they want to hear. It was a one-way street, but he simply focused on finding the truth and reporting it.

There were two Chinese at the base located behind his offices. They broadcast U.S. messages daily to Chicom troops in Korea. Philip and his fellow agents had the task of guarding them during their off-duty hours. One agent, who looked and acted just like a macho caricature of an intelligence professional, tried to show Philip that the 45-caliber pistol he used for guarding the Chinese could not be fired when the barrel was thrust back to a fixed position. The agent was shocked when he shot a hole through his own hand. An angry detachment commander took away his credentials before sending him to the hospital.

An opening became available for an agent on the outlying island of Amami Oshima, and Philip volunteered for it. Amami had a total of seven agents and seventy thousand Ryukyuans, some of whom had captured and beheaded U.S. pilots during World War II. When the war ended, a wise General Douglas MacArthur sent a statement through the Japanese emperor to all residents that U.S. occupation troops were to be treated humanely. The message was understood, and Philip spent one year on the island working quietly with the governor and political and opinion leaders. He had daily radio contact with Okinawa, and once a month a boat arrived with food and mail.

Philip worked from a CIC field office located directly below a Shinto temple. At night it was dreamlike. There was a high Japanese torii arch nearby and behind it a long, rising stairway that reached the temple lit by a silver moon. During the day he sat cross-legged on tatami mats since there were no chairs, drank hot ocha green tea, and interviewed visitors. In the evening he wrote his radio messages and sent them to Okinawa.

Meetings with the governor were usually held at a private restaurant of his choice. The meals were of delicious Japanese food, and hot sake and warm beer with ice in it were served. The governor's favorite drink was habu sake, which was made by placing a deadly habu viper in a sho bottle and letting it float for several months before pouring the drink to develop mutual understanding. He also had to smoke as many cigarettes as were offered. Philip, a non-smoker, learned this when one of his close friends was transferred from the island for not following cigarette protocol.

At the end of his year on the island of Amami Oshima, Philip was transferred back to Okinawa. From there he boarded a troop ship to the U.S. port of Oakland and then went by train to Fort Sheridan, outside Chicago, to be discharged. He took a taxi to his family's house, walked in, and sat on the floor. He found it difficult to readjust to the Midwest, and after talks with his mother they decided that it was now time for him to go to Mexico to learn about the other half of himself.

EXCEPTIONAL WOMAN

Philip's wife Maruja Carrera who gave him love and a complete life

Mexico Disconnect

Philip returned to Mexico City to get to know his father and understand his future. He studied at an American university there with a cohort of military veterans who were part of a generation disconnected from the past by war. Many of them had trekked down the western coast of California into Mexico. They were preceded by a Hollywood group that included Gary Cooper, Tyrone Power, Errol Flynn, and Johnny Weissmuller from Chicago. Later people came like William Burroughs, the writer who under the influence of drugs shot his wife instead of the apple on her head, and Norman Mailer, who lived nearby and was writing *The White Negro*.

Philip soon realized that his own background and the elite Mexican culture he was coming to know were at opposite ends of a spectrum of values. The deepest value contradictions he found were between his father and himself. His father had built his life on money and public recognition. Philip had been raised in a poor family who had never abandoned him, and he knew he would never abandon them. Although he had the son of the Mexican president to escort him through customs at the airport and was introduced to socially prominent young women who wanted to know how many cars his father had, Philip spent his free time delivering food to indigenous people in remote villages and helping flood and earthquake victims.

It became clear to Philip that his dream of knowing his father and earning his love was not realistic. His father insisted that he stop studying and take up a position in business. Philip continued to serve the poor. Their clash reached a peak when Philip's half sister began dating a young man from the conservative Spanish colony in Mexico City and Philip met the young man's sister.

Maruja was different from the upper-class women he had met in the exclusive Mexico City suburb of Lomas Chapultepec. She was strong-minded, beautiful, quite independent, and not driven by money. Philip was received warmly in Maruja's home. His sister was not. His father talked angrily to Maruja's parents, warning them that Philip had come to Mexico to get his money and that he did not intend to give him any. The parents thanked Philip's father for the information and advised him that Philip had not been received in their home on the basis of his bank account. He had been recommended by his father. At Philip's house the wheels of inevitable rupture began to turn.

After an emotional confrontation with his father, Philip decided to leave his house. His father instructed him to first return the gold watch he had given him. Philip gave him the watch—any watch gives the time of day—and departed in a taxi. When he tried to continue his studies at the university, his father sent government agents to force him to leave the country. Philip avoided them, made plans with Maruja, and left Mexico discretely. He visited his family in Chicago and then drove alone across the United States to Berkeley, California, where he shared a small apartment with a U.S. marine who was a fellow veteran and friend from Walnut Creek. He found a position as a labor-relations conciliator in the South San Francisco industrial district and settled down to building his life. Several months later he located an empty apartment on Woolsey Street in Berkley and rented it. He painted the walls, installed shelves, and decorated each room in order to receive and care for his future wife.

A year later, Philip returned to Mexico City and married Maruja at the Church of Perpetuo Socorro in Lomas Chapultepec. Standing at the altar, he did not understand why she had chosen to marry him. She had society's richest and most elegant young men at her fingertips. He assumed he had nothing to offer her, but he knew she was an unusual woman and wanted to share her future with him. After honeymooning in Acapulco, they drove to Berkeley and began to build their life together. Maruja's mother, who had often noticed sadness in Philip, told her in a letter:

> *This boy does not yet know who he is. When he has his own*
> *wife and family he will find out and he will be happy.*

And that is exactly what happened. They lived a unique life alone together in Berkeley. When Maruja was pregnant with their first child they returned to Mexico City. Philip took a position in a firm representing U.S. companies and continued to work with the poor. His life with Maruja began to come together in ways he had never imagined possible. The only thing he needed was to fill the emptiness that his father had left inside him.

His Father's House

Philip had left his father's house once, and now that he was back in Mexico with his wife Maruja he did not intend to return to it. It was there that he had been accused of coming to Mexico in order to get his father's money. But his heart started to change when Maruja told him that his father was sick and alone. His wife had left him temporarily.

Philip hesitated and then agreed to make the visit as a humane act. His father received them at the door to his iron-gated, marble-floored residence. They entered and sat in overstuffed sofas in the large downstairs living room, surrounded by crystal vases, rich paintings, and silver trays. It would have impressed most people.

His father talked about his Sunday outings as a gentleman Mexican charro equestrian. He showed him closets full of expensive charro suits with silver pieces adorning the trousers and silver spurs to match them. He informed Philip that a charro museum in Chapultepec Park was to be named in his honor. As they talked, the conversation moved to the subject of cameras. His father had a large collection and he asked Philip if he had one. Philip lied and said yes.

When the visit ended his father insisted that they come again. Three days later Philip learned that his father had told people that Philip went to the house asking for money and to live there.

As the days passed, Philip thought back to his conversation with Maruja after they had said goodbye to his father.

"Why did you lie when he offered you a camera?" she had asked.

"You don't know my father," he had replied.

Philip had understood his father and the situation correctly. But he had never been taught to hate or be envious, and he hoped that his father would somehow put his own life in order.

Philip realized that in life situations he had to identify and resolve the underlying problems. Otherwise they would poison him. He was beginning to understand how imperfect people really were. They could do almost anything and then justify it in their minds.

When he became strong enough to understand that extreme imperfection was a fundamental part of the human condition he forgave most human behavior. In the process he also learned to forgive himself. His goal was no longer perfection. It was to increase his understanding of imperfection and forgive it in others and in himself. Drop all past resentments. Live in the present. Learn. Move on.

The Mother

Maker of the greatest miracle
Selfless love that shines
Beyond the blindness
Of the ego-driven male

Sacrificing daily
She gave her love quietly
Never conditioning it
For convenience or gain

Formed the child
In her image of love
Taught him
Without resentment

It is a privilege
To have had such a mother
And to see in her
The mothers of all cultures

And to try to be
The man she saw in me

The Father

When his father left him
Without explanation
He blamed himself
And doubted that anyone
Could ever love him
Sensitized by the suffering
He looked desperately
Everywhere for his father
But he had no guide or compass
And he stumbled blindly
Making endless mistakes
Doing foolish things
Wondering how he could ever
Find his place in life
He questioned everyone
And each time he asked
A piece of that person
A thought
An experience
Became a part of him
And one day he met
An African American lawyer
Who had suffered
And understood him
And became his older brother
And he met a remarkable woman
Who became his wife
And gave him the thread of love
To find his way out of the labyrinth
And after time
When their children grew
And questioned him
He found to his surprise
That he could answer them
With knowledge and love

And no hate of the past
Or doubt about the present
And one day he looked into a mirror
And suddenly saw the person
He had been seeking
And the person looking back
Told him without words
That he had become
The father he had lost
So many years ago

Thomas Lucius Berkley

It was a clear day in April in Mexico City, and Philip was at work in his office in a high-rise office building near the downtown business district when Thomas Lucius Berkley knocked and entered. Tom was older, tall, and powerful, and he had the bearing and grace of an African prince. His voice and body were a smooth blend of mature energy.

"Mike gave me your name. Said he would let you know I was coming."

"Yes, I got his note. Glad to see you, Thomas. Please sit down and let's talk."

"Thanks. I got here in a taxi. Didn't know enough Spanish to get him to wait. You speak American English. Where are you from?"

"Chicago," Philip said with pride. He loved his town. "I finished military service in Japan and came here to know my father. He worked in export in Chicago and came back to Mexico to take a position in the petroleum industry."

Philip did not say that his father had abandoned him in Chicago or that the traumatizing experience still affected him deeply. He did not trust men.

"What do you do here?" Tom asked.

"A little bit of everything. Mostly I do opinion research for a group in the United States. How about you? Mike didn't tell me anything except that you were coming."

"That Mike. He's craaazy. Came to my house in a rainstorm to tell me he was fed up with some things in the United States and wanted to find out how he could help me. When he knew I was going to Mexico he gave me your name."

"What do you do in Oakland, Tom? Why did you decide to come here?"

"I have a Mexican restaurant, Casa de Eva. I publish a newspaper. Got a law firm. And I'm president of the Oakland Port Authority. I came down to buy some Oaxacan dishware for my restaurant. And I want to meet Mexican politicos who can give me information for my readers in California. They want to know more about Mexico than the weather and the guided tours. But that would take more explaining than we have time for sitting here," Tom said, looking at his gold wristwatch.

Philip was thoughtful. He could not say to Tom that he had renewed his intelligence ties with a U.S. organization, but he recognized immediately that he could supply Tom with the kind of information he needed. It would take time to work things out, but he realized that he could help Tom.

"Why don't we go to lunch Tom? There's a restaurant called Círculo del Sureste down the street with food from the Yucatan and the ambience is agreeable," Philip said, translating into English the Spanish he now used every day.

"Fine with me" Tom replied, smiling.

They walked to the restaurant and sat down at a square wooden table. A waiter, fat and friendly, brought them two bottles of Negra Modelo beer and two menus. The beer was icy. They ordered *cochinita pibil* and *frijol con puerco* and ate and talked comfortably, although Philip was still cautious. He had the always-present mistrust of the intelligence professional, and below the water lay his underlying mistrust of men. His father was wealthy and successful in the eyes of the Mexican public, a leader in the petroleum industry. A museum in Chapultepec Park was to be named in his honor. But living in his father's house had taught Philip to always look below the surface for the truth.

"Where are you from originally, Tom?"

"DuQuoin, in southern Illinois. But we moved to California when I was small. I ran track for UCLA, and then I got a law degree at Cal Berkeley. Worked in U.S. Army logistics during military service, and after that I set up my own law firm in Oakland."

Philip was surprised. They were communicating with immediate clarity, and the stream of conversation flowed naturally and extensively.

"Tom, do you realize that we both started in Illinois and we were both poor?" he observed. "You chose to make money and I understand why. I chose to serve people who were treated unfairly. When you know me better you will understand why."

"That's good," Tom replied. "The most important thing in life is to understand what is happening. If you don't understand you can't solve and you can't win. You only get one bite at the apple when it goes by. You can't afford to miss it."

Philip continued, "Mike, my U.S. Marine friend from Walnut Creek, went to your house just as you were going to Mexico, and he put us together here. That's a very improbable set of circumstances."

Tom chuckled. "Yes, but we are a couple of pretty improbable people, aren't we? You should be breaking concrete in the Chicago streets, and I should be on the docks in Oakland. Maybe we've got something to do together. We could even end up on the Mississippi like Huck and Jim."

Another surprise for Philip. Tom's imagination was placing them on Mark Twain's river, the Mississippi that Philip had crossed so many times to travel from Chicago to reach his liberal arts college. Twain had been the first American writer with enough sense to recognize the black man as a human being. Philip hated the injustice that African Americans had endured.

"Yes, Tom. Except that it's a long and wide river with lots of currents. It always flows, and at the end it disappears into the sea." Without knowing why, he said, "It's a good idea. But you're the captain. I'll be the apprentice. Maybe I can learn from you how to navigate. Let's do it and see where the river takes us."

Philip did not realize that he had just made a decision that would change his life. He would no longer be alone on the river, blind and isolated.

The Mentor

Tom Berkley was the grandson of four slaves. Major Berkley was the first of the family to reach America. He crossed the ocean as cargo on a slave ship and worked as a laborer on a plantation. He decided one day that he should not to be owned by someone as chattel along with horses and cattle. It was the time of Lincoln and the Civil War. He escaped from the plantation and followed Union troops north along the land edge of the Mississippi River to reach an island facing the town of Cairo, Illinois, where an army officer gave him his freedom and a name. He became Major Berkley. He settled in the nearby coal-mining town of DuQuoin and raised a family. In DuQuoin, Tom's father, Braxton Berkley, worked as a coal miner and labor leader, and his mother was a teacher.

Tom was the seventh son of a seventh son, described in a family book as, "a special person in the generations of the Berkley family." When Braxton moved the family to southern California, Tom worked with Mexican laborers in the Imperial Valley. When the family moved north, Tom signed on as a longshoreman in a port, loading cargo by hand onto ships.

Tom was smart. It did not take him long to understand that there were things to do in life beyond working on the docks. Like Major Berkley he made a choice. He decided to enter mainstream America and earn his share of the "American dream." He had no money, but he was an outstanding athlete and was accepted at UCLA, where he became the world's best hurdler in his time. He studied economics and law, and during his senior year at UCLA Tom wrote a prophetic essay.

> Born black in a white man's country. Twenty-two years a member of a race debased, kept in ignorance, and demoralized by 250 years of slavery. Despised, hated, exploited, and intimidated. But a new Negro is rising. An individual whose thoughts, actions, ambitions, and determination are American. He will accumulate wealth and demand his place in the economic sun. This new Negro will go places. He will give the United States what it needs. He will become a desirable citizen. In the words of my sister Ruby, the writer and poet:

I can succeed. I will succeed.
Nothing is able to hold me back.
I can succeed! I will succeed!
I will not die on the beaten track.

This was the man who became Philip's older brother and mentor. When Tom dedicated a copy of Ruby's book to Philip, he wrote, "You must know about your whole family. Ruby, your and my sister, tells the story of where we came from." Later when Philip studied one of Ruby's poems in the book, he found a line that he would never forget. "I'm learning to trust my brother." Philip knew that Ruby had written that line for him.

Illusion

I grow tired of hearing
Which race or religion or belief
Is better than the rest
Why a particular color
Makes a man smarter
Or better than his neighbor
Why wealth and fame
Cause mindless adoration
And I wonder why men
Keep walking in circles
Grinding at the mill
Of self-justification
Yoked to the ego
Blind to the beauty
Of human potential
Eyeless in a virtual world
Gaping into the past
Demanding that time stop
What will change anyway
In a year or a month or a day
I speak to the young
Who are not yet tainted
And I ask you to be honest
To look inside yourself and
Decide what is worth pursuing
In the changing external world
Where is the real wealth
What will you do to find it
For you will probably get
What you decide to want
As others have
Focused on the self
Building empty lives
Of material adoration
Missing the richness
In going beyond the self
And leading
By serving others

LEADERSHIP

Tom and Phil meet with Mexican President Miguel Aleman

The Challenge

Philip was navigating now on the river of life with his mentor, and he began to organize the itinerary for Tom's return to Mexico. It was not a difficult task. He had the help of the son of a Mexican president, who had worked for Philip's father at the Atzcapotzalco petroleum refinery in Mexico City.

Philip's most vivid recollection of the president's son was at a dinner several years earlier in his father's house. The young man and a friend had arrived at the dinner slightly drunk and looking for more alcohol. When they found a bottle of Courvoisier cognac, the friend, claiming to be a candle, twisted his sparse hair into a knot at the top of his head, poured the cognac over it, and attempted to light it. After that the dinner formalities seemed less important. The son turned out to be a warm and helpful person who simply had too much money and too little character. When he learned from Philip about Tom's impending visit, he arranged a meeting with his father the president and appointments with various government officials.

On a Wednesday evening at his home, a modest duplex in the south of Mexico City, Philip was chatting with his wife Maruja. He would be leaving shortly for the airport to receive Tom. Maruja had become the central person in Philip's life, although he still did not understand why she had chosen to marry him. As the years passed he would go beyond his trauma and understand the depth of her love.

Maruja was smart and perceptive about many things. She knew that Philip was comfortable with the women in her family and that he did not trust men. She sensed that there was something different in him this evening.

"Why is the visit of Tom Berkley so important to you? I have never seen you so enthusiastic about the arrival of a business acquaintance."

"I'm not sure, but I feel that I have finally met a man worth respecting. He has been the world's best at something. And he has suffered and stood above it without losing himself. I have never met a man like him."

Philip kissed Maruja and left for the airport. He found it crowded with international tourists, mostly Americans, coming to stay at American hotels, sit in American bars, and eat in American restaurants.

They would return to the United States to tell their friends that they now understood Mexico.

Philip saw Tom Berkley as he came through the arrival gate. He was dressed in an elegant, dark brown suit with a beige tie and was accompanied by a handsome woman. Tom introduced her.

"This is my wife, Velda, from Walnut Creek. She is also my business partner."

Velda was African American and had Cherokee Indian blood and the blood of the Irish slave master who had loved her grandmother. She was dressed smartly and had a warm smile.

"Hello, Philip. Tom has told me about you. It sounds like you two understood each other very well during his last trip here."

"You're right about us, Velda. Thanks and welcome to Mexico City."

Philip walked the couple to his car at the curbside and drove them to the Hotel Presidente, where Tom had reserved a luxury suite. While Tom registered he suggested to Philip, "Why don't you and I have breakfast tomorrow morning in the hotel?"

"Fine with me, Tom. You're the captain. We can go over the visit schedule then.

Maruja will call Velda, and the women can spend their day together."

Philip already realized that Velda and Maruja were matched in quality and elegance. He knew they would enjoy one another's company.

During the next three days, Tom and Philip met with politicos, business leaders, and newspaper owners. Their most significant conversation was with the Mexican president at his residence in Los Pinos, at the edge of Chapultepec Park. It was near the castle that had been the imperial home of Emperor Maximilian and his wife Carlota. President Lazaro Cardenas had severed that historical tie by moving the residence from the castle to Los Pinos.

When the president received them Philip noticed mutual charisma in the style of the two men. Tom introduced himself in Spanish.

"Mr. President, thank you for receiving us. I have been a fan of your country since I worked with Mexicans in the Imperial Valley in southern California."

"Welcome, Mr. Berkley. I am told that you understand us and that you publish your California newspaper in Spanish as well as English. We need a voice like yours in the United States."

"Thank you, Mr. President. Unfortunately many people in the United States do not know or understand Mexico. They do not even know the cultures and races inside their own country. I am trying to teach them through my newspapers."

"Mr. Berkley, you are a world traveler and a man of vision. You know the problems we face. Overpopulation. Scarcity of water, forests, and air. A lack of jobs here that will generate anger, violence, and crime. Our people will emigrate. The U.S.-Mexico border will become a blur. Our land maps will not reflect our population maps. Emigration will generate clashes between our countries. When our people work in the United States we will blame you for not taking care of them. When your people consume drugs you will blame us for supplying them."

Tom took a deep breath and kept listening.

"We are at the edge of world change. Disconnecting from the traditional past. In some places change will be abrupt and violent. Our challenge is to reduce extremism by building our common interests and the culture of democracy. You are doing this, and I am prepared to help. You are a leader and you come from the people. Your record is clear."

Tom was gratified. The president had understood him and what he was about. When the meeting ended, a bond of understanding and cooperation had been established.

That evening, Tom and Philip talked about what they might accomplish together. Philip decided to write for Tom's newspaper readers. Tom brought up an unusual idea.

"Look, I know you hate money because you saw how it distorts people. I know you want to stay close to the poor. But it is time to put some balance into your life. You ought to learn to work with money. It is bought and sold like any other commodity. Get into the money business. Use it to help people. You can't win the race if you refuse to run."

Tom and Velda left Mexico the next day, but Tom's idea stayed in Philip's mind. He could not escape the logic. It became a challenge to make a major change in his life. He decided to do something about it.

Doing

Doing is the best teacher
Testing you daily
Against the jagged edges of reality
Cutting into your dreams
But not destroying them
Unless you choose to hide
In any of the fashionable escapes

Books teach you
To understand
What you have done
And can do
If you have the will
To read and think and act
And persist

Suffering teaches you
If you let it
If you have the patience
And can stand the pain
It brings you humility
That opens the doors
To wisdom

People teach you
Without knowing it
If you seek them out
And watch and listen
Without resentment
And understand their errors
And occasional epiphanies

And as you search
You may even meet
A mentor
Who helps you find
The hard realities
You must face and solve
To reach your dreams

Oakland

Several weeks after Tom's visit to Mexico, Philip took a morning flight direct to Oakland. When he landed in the Oakland airport he phoned Tom Berkley.

"Tom, I'm on my way to New York. I'm doing what you told me to do. I have to talk to you."

"What? Are you craaazy?"

"No. You were right. I have to find balance."

"Stay where you are. Don't move. I will be with you in twenty minutes."

Tom arrived in his Mercedes Benz, and the two men talked as he drove to his office.

"I'm on our river, Tom. Moving into the money business. I need you to teach me how to do it. I have to be in New York on Thursday for an interview."

At his office Tom assigned an assistant to research the New York merchant bank that Philip would visit. It was the financial arm of a chemicals trading group. It operated in the secondary money market and was internationally rated as honest and astute. Philip was encouraged. Tom gave him an explanation of money markets and offered to continue his coaching until Philip flew to New York. He cleared his schedule, and the two men spent three memorable days together.

During Tom's mentoring, the two men moved around Oakland as brothers. Tom left his Mercedes at home and drove an old Ford T-bird. They breakfasted at Reggie Jackson's favorite grits restaurant and lunched on barbequed ribs at Earl's. Philip was the only Caucasian in the place, and Tom was his older brother. They drove to Tom's Mexican restaurant, Casa de Eva, on Telegraph Avenue near the UC campus in Berkeley. It was managed by a poor immigrant Mexican couple from Guanajuato who would eventually drive the same Mercedes-Benz model Tom used.

In the evening Philip listened to Tom talk on the phone with Andy Young and other African American leaders. He learned of their concerns, which included high employment rates among their young and the need for opportunities to grow.

Tom described his trips to Africa. He had met with officials, donned tribal robes, and was told by his hosts that regardless of the way he dressed they saw him as American.

On the last evening, Tom took Philip to dinner at the elegant Lakeside restaurant atop the Kaiser Building in downtown Oakland. It overlooked the calm waters of Lake Merritt, which sparkled with reflected light. Philip remembered that Henry Kaiser was the entrepreneur who built cargo ships with incredible speed during World War II to help win the war.

Tom was thoughtful as he talked about his life.

"Look around you," he said. "See what I have accomplished. Imagine what I might have done if the rules had been fair."

"Tom, what you have done is incredible by anyone's standards. Very few Americans can match your record: Attorney consulted by presidents in Washington. Founder of the largest racially integrated law firm in the United States. Builder of integrated housing at Berkley Square in Las Vegas. President of the Oakland Port Authority. Founder of a regional California newspaper published in two languages. Member of business and civic boards. Honorary doctorate. Helping countless people grow and advance. What more are you supposed to do or ask for?"

Philip understood Tom's hurt. Tom was the best man he had ever met, a brilliant visionary and world-class competitor who knew how good he was and wanted fair and full results from his efforts.

"Tom, please do not demand too much from life. You have already made yourself the best."

Tom Berkley smiled. He had opened his heart and his dreams, and his younger brother had understood who he was and what he had done.

Philip would never forget those days in Oakland with Tom, and neither would he forget the wisdom and love and consideration he received. He left the next day on the flight to New York. When he interviewed with the merchant banking group, he won the position. He returned to Mexico, and in his first year in the money business he closed loans for over one hundred million dollars.

As the years passed Philip would realize that he and Tom had understood one another the day they met in Mexico City. In a single meeting, Tom began to fill the emptiness left in Philip by his father. He gave Philip honesty and an unmatchable example of what it meant to be a man and a human being. And he gave him goals to reach for as he built his own life.

Berlin

It was a moonlit night in the cold German winter, and he walked briskly along an icy street in West Berlin. His hotel was several blocks behind him, the Kurfurstendamm one block ahead. He was looking for a particular café recommended by the hotel manager, where he could enjoy a steaming hot dinner, drink Alsace wine, and smoke the dark Cuban cigar he brought with him from Mexico City.

His mind and body were tense from the pressures of recent days. Meetings with leaders of the Mexican petroleum industry, the flight to Frankfurt to work with the German bankers, and the arduous process of getting Mexican and German officials to understand one another had all taken their toll.

"Will the Mexicans honor their commitments?"

"Can we trust the Germans?"

A deutschmark loan from Germany to Mexico worth fifty million dollars and he closed it successfully. He, a Chicago street laborer given the opportunity to study at a university, was responsible, though he knew there were other factors. His cultural mix of Northern Europe and Latin America let him see into the thinking and feelings of other people, to interpret their needs in a globalizing world. And the sacrifices made by others in his past were important.

Brisk walking raised his pulse and increased his blood flow. His body felt a need for oxygen. The rush of cold air into his lungs interrupted his thinking and forced him to look outward. He was suddenly aware of his surroundings and noted that he was nearing a dilapidated, dimly lit three-story house. Near the building a woman stood motionless in the cold. She was young, blonde, red-faced, and attractive. As he passed her she said, "Good evening. Where are you going?" It was obvious that she was going nowhere in the icy night, and her words and glances toward the dilapidated building told him the nature of her profession. He smiled and, replied, "Thank you," and continued his walk.

As he turned onto the Kurfurstendamm he saw the jagged remnants of the bombed cathedral—a reminder of the past. He remembered his immigrant German neighbors in Chicago who believed that Hitler would save the old country.

"In Dresden we used to eat only twice a day," they would say. "We slept to kill the feeling of hunger. He gave us hope."

He remembered his mother, abandoned by her unfaithful Mexican husband and forced to take a job in a factory in the Ravenswood district on the industrial north side of Chicago. She worked every day without complaint to feed and raise him, and in the evenings she taught him to read. She gave him books and the world. She never poisoned his mind against his father. Instead she sent him to Mexico to meet him. She wanted to heal her son's scars of absence and help him find a better life. Later when she fell ill suddenly in Chicago, he reached her in time to tell her how much he loved her and to thank her for everything she had done for him.

As he walked along the brightly lit Kurfurstendamm, he remembered the days in Frankfurt. On the morning of the first day he was taken to the inner chamber office of the bank president. The distinguished white-haired gentleman of obvious aristocratic background received him graciously while an associate introduced him as, "The only man from that New York financial group who isn't a Jew." He realized that although Hitler was dead there were still people who refused to bury him.

After the meeting he was driven by a uniformed bank chauffer in a late-model, black Mercedes-Benz sedan to Heidelberg, where he visited the university and the Koenigsitz, a site which let him look down at the city and its people. At lunch he asked the waiter for a telephone directory and in it he found the Germanized family name of the Jewish stepfather who had raised him in the difficult years after his father left. He had been a good man. Philip respected him.

The next days in Frankfurt were occupied with closing the loan agreement. After the signing of official documents there was an elegant luncheon and a series of high-minded toasts to the future. And then he was free to extend his trip to Berlin—he had always wanted to see the truth on both sides of the Berlin Wall.

He arrived in West Berlin late in the evening and registered at a small hotel recommended to him by the banking staff. The next morning he hurried to join a tour group departing the hotel in a bus. After meeting rigid East German checkpoint demands for individual documentation, the bus crossed through the wall and entered the theoretical paradise of East Berlin. The drab buildings, the lack of goods, and the carefully guarded words of the East Germans reminded him of Cuba. Except that Havana was warm and in Berlin the cold was numbing.

And then his walking ended. He had found the café and he entered its warmth and enjoyed the steaming dinner, the Alsace wine, and the Cuban cigar. He relaxed and understood his good fortune.

Hours later, filled with warmth and good food and wine, he retraced the walking route back toward his hotel. When he reached the turnoff street he saw the same woman at the same corner, only now she was shivering and moving her arms to shake off the extreme cold. He approached her and asked, "How much do you charge for one hour?" She quoted a price, which he paid, and they walked together into the dilapidated building, along a narrow hall, and into a small room with a simple wooden bed and a table nearby holding a basin of water. The room was warm, and the woman was no longer shivering.

She sat down on the bed. He remained standing and asked her for a cigarette. He smoked it quickly, thanked her, and left the room. He walked down the hall past a black-mustached man guarding the door and out into the icy night. He did not feel the cold or see the moon or even notice the lights that edged the street leading back to his hotel. He was looking inward and remembering the people who had helped him. He was grateful.

Cuba

Cuba no debe favores
A ninguna extraña tierra
En Cuba todo se encierra
Cuba ha sido un jardín de flores
Ole bien!

Spanish couplet

Philip was asked to visit the island of Cuba as a businessman in order to collect intelligence. Although Tom Berkley's mentoring had given Philip a more balanced life, he was still loyal to the values battle known as the Cold War and he accepted the task.

He remembered a similar Cuban project he had worked on in the past, when in the mirror world of intelligence he had inadvertently penetrated a friendly network. This time he decided to operate in a different way. He recalled that six months earlier he had met a married couple who had been allowed to leave Cuba. They were elderly people who slept on a mattress on the floor of a small apartment in the north of Mexico City. Philip did not believe it was fair that old people leaving Cuba to reach Western democracy should live this way, so he acted without political motivation to remedy the situation.

He went to his rich in-laws, who frequently changed the decor of their home, and asked them to give him their old furniture. They gave have several items, including a bedroom set. He rented a small truck and delivered the furniture to the elderly couple, carrying each piece to their third-floor apartment.

Now he decided to revisit the couple. They told him their nephew was the private secretary to one of Fidel's founding revolutionary comandantes. When he told them he wanted to visit Cuba the couple introduced Philip to their nephew, who arranged the trip. Philip went well-recommended to the Cuban Embassy where he was given a travel visa. It was a single piece of paper, half to be delivered on arrival at the Havana airport, and the other half on departure. He could travel to Cuba and evidence of his trip would never be stamped on his passport.

Next he eliminated all non-business data from his personal notebook, Palm Pilot, and electronic watch. Then he recruited a private-sector German businessman with intelligence experience and a strong desire to do business in Cuba. The German was a witting asset and discreet. His presence would help deflect any suspicion among Cuban counterintelligence officers they might have to deal with. They printed business cards for a non-existent commercial company, using the German's home address and telephone number for their contact information. Then they set dates for the trip.

When the two men arrived at the airport in Havana they were received by Comandante M, who took them to the Hotel Nacional. Rooms had been reserved for them. After checking in and unpacking, Philip walked out of the hotel and into the street, where he knew he could find the truth. In spite of revolutionary doctrine, the prostitutes were busy with their trade and Cuban currency was available in exchange for U.S. dollars at very favorable and illegal rates. He did not accept either offer. He learned that the best Cuban beaches were off-limits to Cubans. They were open only to foreign tourists with money. Stores with high quality food, much of it brought in illegally from Miami, were open only to diplomats and the ruling elite.

The next day the two visitors were taken to the National Palace, where Philip noted that all the security guards were black. At a meeting at the health ministry he saw that all officials were white except for one robust black officer. He asked why and was told that the man managed the Cuban sports program. During his visit he found almost no equality for black Cubans in power circles.

The days that followed were filled by meetings with government officials and industry managers who described in great detail their capacities, needs, and expectations. At the Cuban Central Bank, Philip sat in the lobby facing a huge red-and-black wall mural of Che Guevara, the former head of the Central Bank, in revolutionary dress. The official who received Philip provided extensive data on Cuba's financial condition.

In the evening Comandante M invited Philip to a private dinner at Morro Castle on the east side of the entrance to Havana harbor. Philip remembered seeing it books when in school in Chicago. He enjoyed the Cuban food, the warm breeze, and the privileged view of Havana. The comandante was in good humor. He laughed as he described how Fidel gave him an assignment to organize a circus for the common people. He received funds, found land and an elephant, had a large tent made, and met with entertainers in order to evaluate their performances. He said that he watched in surprise as the balloonist he had interviewed rose steadily into the sky and never returned.

Philip lunched the next day at the Bodeguita del Medio, a popular Cuban restaurant. The walls were filled with signatures above wooden tables which had names carved into them. His guide explained that during the Soviet honeymoon Russians had enjoyed coming here but had always insisted that the Cubans speak in low, attenuated tones. Anyone who understood the expressive Cuban culture would find this impossible.

Philip asked Comandante M to open Ernest Hemingway's house at Finca Vigia for him. Hemingway was a Chicago writer, and for Philip it was a memorable visit. They drove through a protected gate and up a hill covered with heavy tropical vegetation. Inside the house Hemingway's books, hunting trophies, and memorabilia were undisturbed, as was his nearby tower writing retreat. Everything fit the descriptions given to him in Mexico City by Ermua, the stubborn Basque jai alai player who had lived at Finca Vigia and had once told Hemingway, "You may be a great writer, but you do not know anything about bulls."

For Philip the visit was pure nostalgia, and he thanked the Cubans for their courtesy in opening the house to him. The following day he visited Hemingway's favorite Havana bar, the Floridita on Obispo Street. A waiter described how he had often served Hemingway at its mahogany bar. The waiter insisted that Hemingway had invented the daiquiri at the Floridita. He also claimed proudly that his own son now lived in Miami, where he was a car salesman. There was not much revolutionary pride in his comment.

At the end of the week Philip returned to the offices of Comandante M, where he was asked to give a summary of his visit and add personal observations. He began the report by stating that he was probably the only working-class person in the room. His advice, however, was basically conciliatory. He said he realized that the Cubans wanted to work with the United States, but would have to concentrate on Latin American countries and Canada until Washington changed its political stance.

On his last day in Havana, while checking out of the Hotel Nacional, Philip asked the African Cuban bellboy where he could give away a pair of old running shoes. The young man took them for himself and asked for any other items Philip might want to leave behind. He also wanted to know if Philip would visit Cuba again and invited him to be the godfather of his young son. Philip thanked the bellboy, declined the offer, and concluded again that the revolution was not bringing all the results it had promised.

Philip left Havana with considerable amounts of information, documents, and names to evaluate for future contact. The German was pleased too. He had begun to do business with the Cubans.

Carnival

What do you prefer today
Pink cotton candy
Or the roller coaster of reality

Float high above
In the upper circle
Of the double wheel

Walk the tightrope over the abyss
For the applause of the crowd
Enter the House of Mirrors

Choose whatever distortion
Fits your particular need
For the moment

Hide the truth under shells
Con the public with a smile
Watch the clowns

Or leave the show
Go outside and help the people
Find better ways to live

Caves

He sat in the candle-lit church of Czestochowa at the edge of Mexico City and listened carefully when the priest said that if we were not at peace with our brother we should go and find him and care for him.

Philip's mind wandered from the church and down into a barranca nearby. He crossed it and climbed to reach the caves carved into a hill on the other side. Anyone could see them if they wanted to. Tiny smudges of black, entrances to another world—the world of the poor. He remembered the Sacromonte caves in Granada. They were warm, well lighted, brightly decorated, and filled with lively people and music.

He thought about the poor for several days after his evening in the church, and then he called together his wealthy nephews from the Spanish colony. They lived in comfort at the top of the Mexico City economic pyramid. He made a proposal to them, and to their credit they accepted his idea. Each one had to get money from his parents and interview a housemaid in order to understand what the poor ate when they could afford it. He told the nephews, "Come with me next Saturday morning." And they did.

Early on Saturday they went together to a market near the caves. Each nephew had to ask for a large box and then fill it with food he had bought for the poor. Once their boxes were full, the boys carried them, following Philip, in a single file down into the barranca, through weeds and excrement and a small, contaminated arroyo, and up the hillside. On reaching the poor in their dark smudge caves the boys were only to say, "We come to share." They did this well and they learned.

In one cave Philip found a child who refused candy. His teeth were rotted and hurt when he ate sweets. Philip found another boy flushed with fever and coughing from pain deep within his chest. The boy sat on a dirt floor, breathing in wisps of smoke rising from a rustic charcoal stove placed near the mouth of the cave.

After the nephews distributed their food, Philip walked them back down the hillside and across the barranca. He returned to the caves alone. He spoke with the parents of the feverish boy and asked for permission to wrap him in a blanket and take him to a government hospital. The parents accepted, and he carried the boy down the hill and across the arroyo and up the other side to his car, which was parked near the church. He placed the boy carefully in the back seat of the car and drove to the hospital.

At the hospital the doctors were hesitant about receiving the child. They told Philip that the boy was retarded and would not improve. But finally they agreed to accept him.

The following Saturday Philip returned to the hospital with the child's parents. The boy was dressed in well-pressed used clothing, and he rested on a clean hospital bed. The doctor attending him said that he was improving. He was not retarded—he had been suffering from malnutrition.

Warmth

I have been the child
With fingers pressed against the glass
Looking inside the candy store
Its lights bright and warm
Endless rows of sweets
And no way to enter
I have been the shirtless worker
Body against the jackhammer
Shaking and breaking
The hard concrete of the Chicago streets
I have been the dishwasher
The waiter for the rich young students
Unaware of my presence
Or my dreams
I have been the soldier
Crawling in the mud
Sleeping in the rain
Learning to lead
Finding out who I am
I have been the businessman
The consultant with answers
Solving for others and building myself
I have been the teacher
The guide to children

Inside the candy store
And to others
Still standing outside
And I have learned
That suffering brings strength
And the absence of hate brings love
I love all the children
Those inside the candy store
With little desire to learn and grow
And those standing outside
With fingers pressed against the glass
Dreaming and hoping
For someone to show them
How to find the door
I know these children well
I know their dream
And I will help them build it
Again and again
I will open the door
And they will come inside
And learn that they are loved
And they will feel the warmth
And enjoy the sweets
Made for all children

Chicago Revisited

And the end of all our exploring
Will be to arrive where we started
And know the place for the first time

—T.S. Eliot

I return to Mexico grateful
For love remembered
And wisdom received
At the grave of my mother
In Chicago
At the end of a day in autumn

I touched her name
Engraved on cold stone
And I saw from the past
The shy Swedish girl
With golden braids and wide blue eyes
Who gave her life to me

Every day of my time with her
She gave love and kindness and care
And the wisdom of women who know
That men are only little boys
Who play at games of war
And believe that they are men

Her gifts outlasted the hardships we faced
Working in the childhood of our generation
Scandinavians Irish Germans Jews Greeks
Thrown together in a new culture
Without knowing who we were
Or who we would become

And although the son of a president
Would attend me in Mexico

I never gave up my Chicago origin
And the people I loved
And love even more now
Because now I understand

We built our lives on hard realities
And never lost ourselves in comfort
Or the excesses of ego
I am the most fortunate of men
For I used the gifts and finally found
The wisdom to understand them

I pass this knowledge on
To people of all ages
So they will know that when
Hard times come again
In this global century
They can build as we did

I see our new immigrants
Asian Indian Arab Mexican Serb
People who continue to arrive
To build Chicago and the country
With their dreams and sacrifices
And their quiet daily work

And when the comfortable progeny
Of immigrants and the *Mayflower*
Believe that life is a new car
I will be there to tell them
That those who sweat and build Chicago
Are building lives that call for our respect

PHILIP AND MARUJA

Philip and Maruja return to Chicago where everything began.

Mexico

Mexico
Lindo y querido
Ancient oriental culture
In transition

Mixed with the blood
Of conquistadores
And priests and the music
Of Jose Alfredo and Palmerin

People who understand
The feelings that flow
Behind their masks
And are not afraid to cry

You took me in
Gave me love
Taught me my name
Who I am

I love your quiet voices
I know your imperfections
And now you know mine
My heart is yours

Octavio Paz

Where you go you take me
Beyond the edges
Of language and origin
To dreams
Dimensionless

I travel motionless
Destination pales
Before exploration
Meaningless
Until unraveled

The answer
To Buñuel's question
Is that love
Warms the icy waters
Of selfish calculation

Humility is the door
Wisdom the reward
The answer to suffering
Is gratitude
I embrace suffering

Earthquake

The Mexico City earthquake of 1985 was traumatic and not easily forgotten. Death toll estimates ran between fifteen thousand and twenty-five thousand, but no one will ever know the true number. It is buried in the rubble along with official political statements.

On the morning of September 19, Philip was in his house at the edge of the city breakfasting with his wife, Maruja. At 7:19 AM they felt sudden oscillatory waves from the ground below them and then harsh trepidatory shudders. Philip turned on the TV. The channels were dead. He calmed Maruja, slipped into a jogging suit and running shoes, and went outside to inspect the area. He saw no visible damage and concluded that the effects of the quake were limited. Maruja, on the other hand, predicted that the damage would be considerable.

Philip showered, changed into a business suit, and drove to a meeting in an office building in the Polanco district next to the Red Cross building. He arrived early, walked over to the Red Cross, and saw hundreds of injured victims being carried from strings of volunteer taxicabs into emergency treatment rooms. He realized the extent of the tragedy, took off his jacket and tie, and helped unload victims and medical supplies. After several hours he returned home, changed back into a jogging suit, and went to the nearby Anahuac University, where an emergency care center had been set up. He found wealthy students organizing volunteers into rescue teams and setting up a radio network that would be a key communications link in managing the tragedy.

At the university he joined a group leaving to dig victims out of collapsed buildings near the medical center on Cuauhtemoc Avenue. The avenue was lined with ambulances, military trucks, and field kitchens serving hot food. Army helicopters were landing nearby to evacuate injured people. Philip and his team were assigned to a fifteen-story building which was now only three stories. They began working with picks, shovels, and hacksaws to remove wreckage and search for survivors.

Philip worked until late afternoon and then began a long walk back toward Reforma Avenue in order to observe firsthand the realities of the quake. He saw an entire school that had been picked up and deposited in the middle of a street. Buildings were toppled, sandwiched, or shaved open. Their upper floors resembled stage sets with tables and dishes strewn about and curtains fluttering in the wind. On the ground in front of him were books, toys, a doll, shoes, a pillow—scattered signs of interrupted lives.

He reached another street that now rose like a rollercoaster ramp, veering upward and around a corner to nowhere. Hotels and residences were piles of rubble and dust. It was a war zone, and people in it huddled in quiet groups. He did not see or hear a single case of loud, disruptive behavior. The dignity and humanity of the Mexicans would become an unforgettable memory.

Days later when Philip reflected on the experience he saw it as a unique moment. Social hierarchies and selfishness had disappeared. People had achieved through suffering what they refused to do in their comfortable, isolated lives.

TEXAS

Philip with Texas Governor William Clements,
heading the State of Texas Business Development Office in Mexico City

Globalization

To William Butler Yeats

Permanent departure
From the past
In the widening gyre
Of a virtual world

Measuring the results
Of Greek civilization
Krutch asked
Were they good or bad?

The answer depended
On where you stood
Where your place was
In the hierarchy

Terkel asked
Who built the pyramids?
And he answered
The People

While at the top
Everyone answered I did
Alone and honestly
Always honestly

Power converges at the top
While at the base
The ceremony of innocence
Is drowned

The poor know
Their needs
Will not be met
By globalization

Or Grecian dreams
As the vortex deepens
And the gap widens
And the center cannot hold

Power

at the top
all mafias meet

and deal
and decide

and wink

and teach the People
to obey the law

the gap widens
the game never ends

Cancun and the WTO

The world focuses on Cancun
Its leaders gather to calculate
The future of the Poor
In goods and services
Globalphobics arrive
They have come to fight
For media space
And a few dreams
Among them a foreign leader
Disciplined and intense
Lies to his people at home
I will not attend
Arrives ahead of the rest
Prepares his role
And during the show
Wearing a bright-colored shirt
And a broad hat to hide
His face and his intentions
Leaps out from the crowd
Scales the wire perimeter fence
And once atop it unclasps
A red Swiss Army knife
And plunges the blade into his chest
This is his third attempt to die
At major international events
This time he succeeds
The blade pierces his heart
And he falls dreamlike to the ground
Bleeding and encircled by
Mexicans who are past masters of
Sacrifice and human sentiment
In matters of the heart
What does this act mean to them?
What does it have to do with life?
They left ancient Aztec ritual
Centuries ago
They will go home
Pray for the deceased
And quietly consider him a fool

Danzón

The peacock struts in warm sunlight on summer-green grasses in the sculpted gardens of Las Mañanitas in Cuernavaca. The peacock is fat and elegant, and it moves comfortably among the people relaxing in the sun.

Minutes away in the town's central square, slender couples of modest Indian origin dance quietly on dark volcanic flagstones around the proletarian statue of Jose Maria Morelos, defender of the poor. The couples glide and pivot like mechanical dolls, guided by the music of the danzón, its tempo always increasing.

Nearby two canvas tents shelter workers who hand out tracts and posters directed against Mexico's new democracy. An electronic box in one of the tents blares a loud Orwellian message:

> *Tacos made of fraud. Tacos made of fraud. Made by the*
> *president and his new spurious candidate. Examine them*
> *and decide. Otherwise you will be forced to swallow them.*
> *Tacos made of fraud.*

The few who stop to listen are poor, uneducated peasants. They know nothing of the electoral process or its issues. They have heard about a new authoritarian candidate from the south who calls himself their savior and teaches them to hate upper-class Mexicans. He justifies his radical positions by saying they are steps needed to liberate the pueblo and purify the country. He seeks to intensify the social contradictions that abound in Mexico and calls for the destruction of Mexico's new democratic institutions. He proclaims himself the true future leader of Mexico.

The outgoing president is a well-meaning idealist. In the name of peace and democracy he refuses to apply the law against illegal actions by the candidate from the south and his followers, and he does not always protect the legal rights of innocent citizens. The conservative presidential candidate who will replace him will have six years to bring forty million poor Mexicans into the economy. During these six years many more children will be born.

Everyone knows the danzón never stops. Its tempo always increases.

The Savior

For many years I did not understand that Mexico would eventually be forced to face its own contradictions. When I arrived there, Mexico was a perfect world if you lived in the privileged classes. At that level people were cultured, well dressed, well traveled, and almost everyone knew one another. The poor were humble, dark-skinned, shabbily dressed, and quiet. I watched these two Mexicos living side by side, each pretending the other did not exist. The rich told me there was no poverty in Mexico. The poor told me nothing could be done about the blindness of the rich because they had never been poor.

My work was to track political and social change in Mexico by dealing with people of all backgrounds and beliefs. One day a respected friend advised me that a political extremist rising in the southern state of Tabasco wanted to become president. He was an agitator who knew how to work crowds and the street, a place that elitists often did not want to understand.

Several weeks later I attended a meeting of businessmen at the Hotel Marriott in Mexico City. The man from Tabasco had been invited to speak. During his talk he presented himself as an understanding leader who would work cooperatively to build the business sector in Mexico. When questions were taken from the floor, I asked him why we should believe that he had given up his radical views and would now support a balanced economic system. He replied with comforting words that anyone could have invented for the moment. Because I knew his background I did not believe him. Ideologists, regardless of what they say, do not give up their inner beliefs. To my surprise the businessmen accepted his story and scolded me for confronting him.

Again and again I heard this leader claim to represent the best interests of the poor. I assumed this meant he would work to relieve their suffering. At a meeting with one of his key assistants I proposed that we work through his party to bring family planning programs to the poor. Overpopulation was and still is a potential bomb in Mexico. The poor and the entire country were suffering its consequences. The assistant's reply to my suggestion astonished me. He said, "We do not want to help them solve their problems. We want them unhappy. That is the only way they will march for us and bring the changes we want."

Because of this attitude I chose not to support the leader or his party. He talked about the poor. I came from them, and I could not make them suffer in order to serve the vague greater goals of theoretical ideologists.

There was another problem. The leader was an authoritarian. He gave orders based on his own homegrown political strategies. It was clear that as president he would initiate a one-man rule. I had dealt with dictators of both the left and the right during the Cold War. Now once again I saw the trappings of dictatorship in the name of the people. His ideas ran counter to my basic belief that people should be free to work for change but not to take away the legal rights of others. I saw ideological conflict as a matter of values. Mexico was moving into a values conflict, and the process would last for decades.

During the ensuing presidential campaign I heard the leader constantly exacerbate the gaps that existed between haves and have-nots. He intensified his attacks on Mexico's emerging democracy. Businessmen and the public were shocked at first but finally began to understand that they were dealing with an Orwellian practitioner of doublethink who manipulated the uneducated masses and had a hard core group of true believers to support him. If he became president they realized he would install the kind of extremist government already operating in several countries of Latin America where democracy had failed to deliver economic justice to the poor. The leader would eventually lose his presidential bid, but like all ideologists he continued his attacks. Mexico had ignored its rich-poor gap for centuries. Now it would have to face and resolve its contradictions.

The Tower

There is no greater satisfaction in life than serving people. When we have that dream and make it a reality we change ourselves and we change the world.

—Don Ernesto Flores Maldonado

As the years passed Philip became increasingly aware of how powerfully Tom Berkley had impacted his life. Tom had never stopped moving ahead and was always building himself into a better man. Philip learned that he had to do the same. He decided to upgrade his strategy by serving on boards and as a mentor to young leaders. He began by serving on university and public-service boards. He soon found himself consulting for a Mexican family real-estate group which sought to modernize its business structure and processes.

Philip spent several months studying the group's operations, family members, and staff executives. He had to understand the people behind the group's decisions. He then recommended the formation of an advisory board which would include family, executives, and independent members. He was named to the board and brought in the former CFO for IBM in Latin America as an independent board member. He mentored the family participants individually, put the general director into a business school program, listened to executives at every level, and concentrated on motivating the group to use its potential and work as a team.

The group had problems which originated from old-fashioned, family-based management. It also had an unusual advantage—it owned seventy million square feet of undeveloped land in Mexico City and the Valley of Mexico. It was a land bank unmatched by other Mexican property owners. The origin of the land ownership was a story in itself.

The group's four sons had been raised by an unusual father. Don Ernesto was born into a large, traditional Mexican family of modest origin and limited resources. He began to work at age thirteen and studied commerce at night. Because he worked most of the day his grades were low. But he was persistent and never failed a course. He sold construction materials with his father and two brothers during the week, and on Sundays he bought and sold blocks of bus tickets. He used his profits to go to the local cinema with his friends. Later in life he said that he always enjoyed those simple moments he had worked to earn.

When World War II began, Mexico entered a construction boom. Don Ernesto sold tires to the industry and then structural steel. In the 1950s his father was offered a small piece of land in the Mexico City suburb of Santa Fe. Father and son bought the land and mined it for gravel and sand, which they sold as building materials. Mining was originally done with pick and shovel. Sophisticated machinery was installed later to modernize the process.

With time Don Ernesto realized that the pieces of land they had bought and mined could eventually become sites for major buildings. Although he never built in the Santa Fe area, Don Ernesto did put up his first office building in the south of the city.

When Don Ernesto retired due to age his sons took over the business. Each had a different style, but they remained united in their common real-estate interests and their family values. While mentoring them Philip realized that the oldest brother, Ernesto, was serving as president only because of family tradition. He was capable and firm, but he had less interest in land development than his younger brother Andres, who had a passion for development and wanted to build. Philip suggested discretely to Ernesto that he consider resigning, remaining on the Board but letting his younger brother Andres take his place. Ernesto agreed and Andres was named president.

Under the leadership of Andres, a team of family members, professional executives, and experienced independent board members began to coalesce. But it lacked a specific target. One day at a private meeting Andres found himself forced to choose between two client buyers of prime family lots in Santa Fe. Philip suggested that he not sell and instead reflect on his options. Andres, who had always wanted to take the business to the next level, decided to build a major office tower on the property. Philip helped Andres assemble a team of young Mexican professionals to carry out the project. The tower would be built, and Andres and his brothers would fulfill their father's dream.

As the tower project progressed, Philip saw positive changes in the team members involved. They cooperated and shared their knowledge and experience. Several of them enrolled in graduate-study programs. Andres studied at a nearby university with his son Diego. It became apparent that besides constructing an office tower each participant was building his own tower of inner personal growth. Don Ernesto's example was affecting the next generation.

Don Ernesto was a man who understood life, had vision, and never stopped trying to grow. He based himself on values that included fairness, honesty, simplicity, resourcefulness, and persistence. When he died he left a clear example of what we can do when we choose to build and never stop trying to serve the world around us. Don Ernesto's legacy also included a surprising number of social projects and schools that he had built quietly without asking for recognition. His sons would continue this tradition.

Plateau

Mentored by Tom Berkley and helped by a good brother-in-law and a few close friends, Philip made a sizeable amount of money in business and finance. He decided, however, not to follow the path to wealth. Although he knew quality people who had followed that path, he also saw others who were blind and unhappy. He understood the risk of building a life focused on money and decided instead to continue serving the poor.

He researched to identify social action programs needed in Mexico. He found numerous qualitative problems and one major underlying quantitative problem—overpopulation. He then located a private-sector Mexican population planning organization and volunteered to become the assistant to its president. They worked together for several years with outstanding women volunteers at all economic levels. Together they built the largest and most successful family planning program in Mexico, servicing more than two million people.

He also found and worked in projects reaching the rural poor, flood and earthquake victims, street children, students, and young people seeking educational opportunities. Along the way he recruited many good Mexicans who wanted to help their people. They did not come from a cultural tradition of volunteerism and were glad to find out how they could participate and make a difference.

He joined a project for earthquake victims which had been initiated by the U.S. Embassy. It was later privatized and expanded to help people in rural areas develop schools and health, medical, and community services. In one village he found people living without water. To finance the construction of a water system, he looked for support among the rich. Only one person responded. He made a large, anonymous donation and the water system was built. The donor showed compassion for the suffering of others and was, by the way, gay.

Realizing the value of education, Philip worked as a volunteer to build the Mexico program of an international university. He oriented students, gave talks on values, studied with them, served as a board member, and became chairman of the university's advisory board.

He found opportunities to mentor individuals. He helped a housemaid's brother into a university degree, an African from Ghana into a medical degree, and young executives looking for ways to build balance in their business and family lives.

He kept his door open and listened to anyone looking for ways to grow. He created a plateau where anyone could rest, exchange ideas, and move on in life. He discovered that their happiness was his happiness. They gave his life a dimension he never could have bought with money.

The River to the Sea

On a December day in Mexico City, Philip received the sudden news that Tom Berkley had died in Oakland. He and Maruja flew there to be with Velda and to participate in the ceremony to honor Tom. Philip found himself in the lobby of the Waterfront Hotel in Jack London Square, remembering Tom. The day outside was cold. Philip leaned forward to hear the words of the television reporter who appeared on the screen. She was Chinese American and very pretty. She said:

> "Mayor Jerry Brown has declared today to be Tom Berkley Day in Oakland. The memorial ceremony for Mr. Berkley, newspaper publisher, lawyer, and former president of our Oakland Port Authority, will begin at noon in the Simms Auditorium. Six hundred people from across the United States and other countries are expected to be there to honor the life and accomplishments of Mr. Berkley. Mayor Jerry Brown and San Francisco Mayor Willy Brown will be among the speakers. We in Oakland will miss Mr. Berkley."

Philip heard the sadness in her voice and it reached inside him. Tom had been his brother and mentor for years. He loved Tom deeply and missed him already.

He walked outside to Jack London Square. Through a slight mist he could see the moored USS *Potomac* belonging to President Franklin D. Roosevelt, where Velda had given birthday parties for Tom. Beyond it were the giant cranes that Tom had brought from China to move massive cargo containers to and from the ships of the world. Philip stepped into the lobby of the port authority building and saw a life-sized photo of Tom. There was a note next to it expressing regret at his death and stating what he had done for the people of Oakland.

"He was our best," the African American receptionist said. She spoke quietly and with pride. "We are going to name our newest and biggest crane after him. When he brought it here it was so huge they had to clear the bridge for it to enter our port."

Philip thanked her warmly for the information and went outside again to the square. It was empty. He walked over to the statue of Jack London. Instead of facing the sea as the writer had, it looked landward to the people who passed it daily. Etched into the base of the statue was the statement: "The proper function of man is to live, not exist. I will use my time." Philip understood the depth of the words. He had learned them from Tom, and on each trip to Oakland he made it a point to see the statue and read the message again.

When Philip reentered the hotel lobby, he heard a friendly hello. He looked toward the voice and saw Kurt McGrath standing near the registration desk, talking with Tom Bradley, the former mayor of Los Angeles. Kurt was a leading businessman in southern California. Both men had been on Tom Berkley's UCLA track team. As students the three had worked together digging rocks out of farmland in order to pay the college expenses not covered by their athletic scholarships. Tom was the best athlete of the three and would tease the Los Angeles mayor, insisting that he had to move faster as a runner and later as a politician. Tom had been best man at Kurt's wedding in Arizona, but after the ceremony a restaurant proprietor had refused to serve Tom. Kurt never forgot that.

"Hi, Philip. Glad to see you here. How is Mexico City?" Kurt asked.

"Great. Business is expanding. We have the silver medal in population, and we are going for the gold. Hello, Mr. Mayor. How are you, sir?"

"I am fine, and I am glad we are all here to pay our respects to Tom," Mayor Bradley replied, shaking Philip's hand.

Philip remembered how Tom laughed the day he introduced the mayor at a fundraiser in Los Angeles, explaining that during their UCLA track days the mayor had charged him ten cents for each ride to the campus in his old jalopy. Tom used to say it wasn't much sugar for a dime.

"You certainly were a great set of athletes for UCLA," Philip said.

"It is good of you to remember us as we were," Kurt replied. "Even though you are a lot younger we might consider making you an honorary member of our team."

Philip smiled. He was already on Tom Berkley's team. He had been running with Tom for years and had told him repeatedly, "I will always run with you. You were and are the best in the world. I never expect to catch you, but I will never stop running with you." Tom and Philip understood each other as brothers. That was what counted.

"Thank you, gentlemen. It would be an honor anytime. I have to leave now to meet my wife. I look forward to seeing you at the ceremony."

Philip walked through the hotel lobby and entered the cafeteria, which was built on pilings over the waters of the port. He saw Maruja and Velda huddled over a table. They were in the same continuing conversation they had started when they first met in Mexico City. Tom had always said, "We married two high-powered women. We have to run."

Philip kissed both women, Velda first. "I guess you two don't really have much to talk about," he said.

"Philip, how can you say that?" Velda replied. "You know we always have a lot of things going on between us." Velda had never stopped being Tom's business partner. She still made things happen at the offices of the newspaper Tom had founded. During their courtship Tom had told her, "Marry me and we will go twice as far in half the time."

They had done exactly that.

Maruja was truly beautiful, and the warmth and charm of southern Spain shone in her as she hugged Philip. "Velda is handling the situation very well," she commented. "She wants everything to be the very best today for Tommy. I will stay with her and we will meet you at the auditorium."

Philip accepted the offer and left the women. The ceremony was still several hours away, and he wanted to be alone in his room with the past. He took an elevator to the third floor, and when he entered his room he locked the door, loosened his tie, and slouched into a soft chair. He picked up Ruby's book that Tom had given him when they started out on their river together.

As he read his mind relaxed and crossed the line between reality and dream. It was night and he found himself on the river with Tom, who was guiding the raft. In the sunlight the waters had been calm and the trip a magnificent adventure, but now in the pale light of the moon he could see turbulence around him and the waters began to engulf them.

Tom was strong, but he was tiring as the raft pitched and tossed in deepening currents. Heavy rain began to fall around them. The raft moved rapidly toward a dark cavern, and when it entered the cavern

Philip realized that Tom was no longer with him. The cold water striking his face told him that he had to guide the raft himself as it moved toward a sunless sea.

He was not afraid. He knew that Tom would be with him. When he awoke he knew what he would say at the ceremony.

Remembrance

Stepping through the doors of Oakland's spacious Calvin Simms Auditorium, Philip found himself awash in a bright sea of life. There were African Americans, many in tribal robes, Japanese, Chinese, Mexicans, Jews, and Anglos. Lawyers, businesspeople, judges, teachers, and artists had been brought together by Tom Berkley. They mingled and chatted with one another and with special guests Willy Brown, the mayor of San Francisco, and Jerry Brown, the mayor of Oakland, who would make a surprise announcement during the ceremony. Printed programs were distributed which described Tom Berkley's life and philosophy and included a poetic quote from Dickens:

> *And can it be*
> *That in a world so full and busy*
> *The loss of one creature*
> *Makes the void in any heart*
> *So wide and deep that nothing*
> *But the width and depth of eternity*
> *Can fill it*

An African American minister stood and gave a prayer of invocation. People were welcomed, and then a film montage of Tom Berkley's life was shown. Tom was there with presidents Kennedy and Carter, the presidents of Mexico, and with Andy Young, Willy Mays, and Josephine Baker. He was pictured with Russians on a ship in Vladivostok and with Arab leaders in Jordan. Then speakers began to recall how Tom Berkley had impacted their lives.

Congresswoman Barbara Lee said, "The world has lost a giant of a man. A brilliant leader. A champion for justice. A world citizen who loved all cultures."

Newspaperman Bill Hughes said, "A coal miner's son and a longshoreman who struggled for an education and never lost his humanity or his fervent desire to improve the human condition, especially for the less fortunate."

Law partner Mas Yonamura commented, "He was a star who made the UCLA basketball team and was never allowed to play. He coached me into law school."

Law school Dean Debra Madison said, "He was a light in a tunnel of darkness. He made you go the extra mile and he did it with a twinkle in his eye."

Dorothy Muller said, "Tom empowered you. He made you stand on your own two feet. He never let you say 'I can't.'"

Congressman Ron Dellums stated, "Tom was a visionary, a globalist, a teacher. He heard the thunder."

Attorney Donald Ray Hopkins said, "Tom Berkley ranks among all the great leaders of every hue and ethnicity that this country has ever produced."

Then the two special guests stood up to speak. San Francisco Mayor Willy Brown said, "You will hear from the 'light Brown,' but first let me tell you that if you never shook the hand of Tom Berkley you missed something. He was a Renaissance man with a vision for a better world. He wanted to make Oakland the major container port on the west coast of the United States. He stole the entire shipping industry from San Francisco and moved it to Oakland."

Oakland Mayor Jerry Brown said, "Tom Berkley was a great leader and we will remember him. He was a newspaper publisher. We will establish a scholarship program for young African American journalists. We will change the name of the street that goes by his office. It will be named Tom Berkley Way, and it will intersect with Martin Luther King Way in the heart of downtown Oakland."

Philip remembered that the new Tom Berkley Way would pass a bank that had refused to lend to him. Tom's name would now be on the bank's stationery.

Then it was Philip's turn to speak.

Gratitude

"I came here to thank Tom Berkley for the example he gave me and the way he affected my life. I spent years looking for a man I could truly respect and admire, and when I met Tom I knew almost immediately that he was that man. We understood each other and for some reason, without telling me why, he invited me to travel with him on his river of life. He said we probably had something to do together, and it wasn't about business or money or power.

"I listened to Tom and I knew he was telling me the truth. I signed on for the trip and together we traveled in Mexico City, Cuernavaca, Manzanillo, Oakland, and New York. Some of our trips were on the river and some were inside the heart. I understood later that our greatest trips were in the heart. And with the size of Tom's heart our trips were enormous and endless.

"We are here today describing what Tom Berkley gave us. For me it was an example and guidance and love. He always helped me in spite of his own hurts—and there were a lot of them. He once took a client of his law firm to a restaurant less than a mile from his office and was refused admittance. As a track competitor representing the United States in the hurdles, he was the world's best during his time and yet was not allowed to sleep in an American hotel with his fellow athletes.

"What kind of a man would take this mindless punishment and still open his heart to people who needed him? Only an unusual man. And we all know what an unusual man Tom was.

"Tom Berkley has left us. What do we intend to do now? Give speeches and go home? That is just too easy. The answer lies inside Oakland's port. Near the waterfront there is a statue of Jack London, placed there to recognize the writer's accomplishments. There is a large, empty space in front of the port authority building where Tom served as president. There should be a statue of Tom Berkley in that space. To recognize what he accomplished. Tom was a visionary, a giant, and one of the great leaders the United States has produced. When will we recognize Tom Berkley and honor him with this statue?"

Evening

On the evening of the same day, Philip and Maruja drove up into the hills of Oakland to the Berkley home near the great Mormon temple. They would be with Velda and a group of close friends. The day had been long and tiring, and now it was time to rest and reflect. The quiet group was multiracial and multicultural. It included people from Africa, Spain, Ireland, Mexico, Sweden, Israel, and Syria. They sat together in an elegant living room with African icons placed in eye-catching locations. An intricate latticework of wood and delicate rice paper set off a space close to the living room. In it was a piano. Nearby an African American woman and her Jewish companion sang "Amazing Grace."

After talking with several people, Philip walked outside to the balcony. He had seen it many times in a photo of Dr. Bernard Lafayette, who was married to Velda's cousin. He was one of the eight young, black college students described by writer David Halberstam as leaders of the civil rights movement in the 1960s. They changed U.S. history.

From the balcony Philip had a broad panoramic view and could see out to San Francisco Bay. Days earlier Velda had made a quiet trip into the bay on a small boat to scatter Tom's ashes. Tom had reached the sea that Major Berkley had crossed generations ago. It was as Tom and Philip understood it would be when they started their river trip together in Mexico City.

At the Oakland edge of the bay, the giant cargo cranes Tom had brought from China stood silhouetted high in the night sky. President Roosevelt's USS *Potomac* rocked gently nearby against the pier close to the port authority building. Far below and to the right, the doors of the Hastings Law School were closed. The stadium was empty. The presses of *The Oakland Post* were silent.

Philip asked himself what the moment meant. To him it meant that Tom had given him a thread of life and he had woven it into something valuable, something that would continue to grow long after the river disappeared into the sea. It meant that he had to keep doing what he believed in—keep building his values and using them whenever he was blinded by the contradictions and superficiality of life.

Philip reflected on all the gifts that Tom had given him since the first day when they talked in the restaurant in Mexico City. He set a magnificent example, gave brilliant insights, and offered the love of an older brother who understood his suffering and never failed him. Philip had found in Tom Berkley the man he was looking for, and now he knew that with Tom's help he would try to become that man himself. He would never stop.

Philip wanted to shout his gratitude across Oakland and the bay. He wanted to reach everyone who had been helped by Tom Berkley and ask them when the statue of Tom would be placed in the empty square in front of the port authority building so that everyone could remember him and thank him for what he had done for them during his life.

The White Man's Burden

We lived alone
In our own closed world
And now we search blindly
For the thread to lead us
Out of our perplexity

China works and rises
The Mexican enclaves
Grow ever larger
Amsterdam becomes Muslim
While the West ages and wanes

Since Copernicus and science
And Nietzsche killed God
And the Great Wars
Killed the dreams
Of Western civilization

We managed the world
For money and might
Without understanding it
Ignored its cultures
Now threatening ours

Huntington believes
We have met the enemy
And they are us
While George leads the blind
Charge downhill

And Alice
Through the looking glass
Tells us we must run
Always faster
To remain in the same place

The Princess of Pop

On the road to fame at eight
She made it at eleven
In the instant electronic media world
Of her virtual generation.
Princess of the dying West
Drugged and often delirious
She doesn't not know why
Her adoring fans cry
While she writhes on her stretcher furious.
Accustomed only to those excesses
That some would call success
No magic kiss of a stalwart prince
Will bring back traditional bliss.
Pray for her
Her mother says
But who is prepared to pray
In her virtual generation
Of secular adoration
What would the enlightened say?

September 11

On the Friday afternoon before September 11, 2001, Philip was at the Canadian Embassy in Mexico City interviewing a friend who was an intelligence officer. Philip was no longer intel-active, but he read extensively and knew that Muslim extremists had tried and would continue to try to penetrate the United States in order to damage it. He understood from his years in counterintelligence that true believers did not give up their goals. Ideology canceled logic. Today he was trying to learn what controls the Canadians were using to detect illegal crossings into the United States. They had already caught one Muslim extremist trying to enter. Why would there not be more?

Philip started the conversation by thanking the Canadian for his country's help during the Iranian takeover of the U.S. Embassy in Tehran in 1979. That event, ten years before the end of the Cold War, marked the beginning of the new terrorist war. According to newspaper reports, the Canadian Embassy in Tehran had provided a safe haven for U.S. Embassy personnel and later escorted them out of the country, protecting them with Canadian passports and documentation.

Philip's Canadian friend was an intelligence professional and cooperated with him. He reviewed northern border controls and pointed out that Canada was not responsible for the U.S.-Mexico border. Philip knew that the southern border was a sieve for illegal entry. Mexican women working illegally in the United States came home to visit their families, knowing which border points they could wade across to return to their U.S. jobs. Mexican men who wanted to spend Christmas with their families in Mexico simply turned themselves in to U.S. immigration officers in order to get free transportation home. After the holiday they would cross back into the United States to return to the illegal jobs waiting for them. Philip remembered that years ago he had pointed out to a U.S. ambassador the probable future flow of an uncontrollable mass of illegal immigrants into the United States. The ambassador had laughed at him, calling his prediction a gross exaggeration.

The Muslim extremists were driven by an ideological agenda. They had announced repeatedly their hatred of the secular West and of the United States in particular. On that Friday afternoon in the Canadian

Embassy, Philip concluded that the extremists would continue to infiltrate the United States. He did not know until after the following Tuesday, September 11, how much factual intelligence had been ignored by U.S. authorities. It was the December 7 scenario all over again.

The Ape

Genetic man
Rises from the ape
Occasionally
While modern man
Seeks by logic alone
To understand people
Though his first need
Is to understand himself
He speaks and does not hear
And believes when he lies
To justify why
 He must be right
Wandering like a blind god
On a comic stage
Avoiding mirrors of truth
Entangled in endless webs
Of ambition and ego
And the war for survival
Already underway

Sand

The waves wash in and fade away
Like the pulse of a dying man
Their message etched
In infinity
Among the grains of sand

Why do we understand so late
And not earlier in the day
When the sun enhances
Our timeless trances
As we dream at the edge of the bay

Where are the men who came with us
To dull the effects of war
Some are dead
All are gone
As we walk the silent shore

Seeking eternity
In the stars
Overlooking the way
Hidden among the grains of sand
In Santa Lucia Bay

Domenech

Empujad al mar mi barca
Con un levante otoñal
Y dejad que el temporal
Desguace sus alas blancas

—Joan Manuel Serrat

After a life of wisdom and kindness and grace, Philip's dear friend Jose Maria died and in one day became a handful of ashes in a small urn. His death was caused by smoking, which produced the emphysema that cut his breathing, clogged his lungs, required him to spend days in bed, paralyzed and collapsed his intestine, and forced an emergency operation. Finally his weakened heart stopped beating.

During a brilliant career Jose Maria carried out successful high-level intelligence assignments in places that no one will ever know about or appreciate. He was a valuable man, an Argentine, a Catalan, and a Mediterranean gentleman. Philip was grateful to Jose Maria for sharing his wisdom and culture during long afternoon lunches and conversations in quiet restaurants in Mexico City and for his kindness during those times spent together.

Philip reflected on the death of Jose Maria and found himself on the river of life moving inexorably toward the sea. He missed Jose Maria and his African American older brother, Thomas Lucius Berkley, who departed in an earlier winter.

The Tree of Life

From the final mass for RP Jesus Lizarbe (Chuchin)

Wisps of gray ceremonial smoke
Rise around the Tree of Life
In the church of Santa Monica
And her saintly African son Agustin
Murmuring priests now kneel and pray
For their late brother Jesus Lizarbe
The god of love receives Chuchin
And pardons and heals us all
In an urn beneath the Tree of Life
Lie the ashes of Chuchin Liberio
Humble breaker of many rules
Who never spoke badly of anyone
And served us with simplicity
Tumor pressing on his brain
Shuffling walk and blinded eyes
Erratic talk and odd behavior
Gave us love and achieved in death
The dignity seldom received in life
Goes now to God and carries our love
We offer thanks and we miss him already

Marati

He saw in a moment
What would always be
As an orange disk
In a sunset of fire
Fell into the silver sea

He followed it down
And left behind
Faint shadows hewn
On the pale gray face
Of a waning moon

Life

A puff of dust
In the cosmic wind
A flickering light
In the night of creation

Alive for moments
Filled with errors
And a few
Epiphanies

In the hearts of those
Who learned
To love and pardon
One another

These words will remain
When all the selfish
Acts of ego
Are turned to dust

Mist

Embedded now and encased forever
In an amber moment of time
Surrounded by sounds of empty talk
And the silence of a dying child

Kaleidoscope bits of colored glass
Form multiple patterned illusions
Reflected against an obscure mirror
And the vanishing mist of life

If life is a moment what should we do
Before the mist disappears
In unseen arcs of curving space
And the liquid clocks of time

Listen Closer

The rustle of leaves in living trees
As the breath of God passes through them

The scent of sweet green cut grasses
Where tiny life forms gestate quietly

The flow of water from the cleft in the rock
Guarded by xanas* and the Celtic mother

Acts of creation from love and the heart
Words that remind us to hold the present

As we rush ahead
Through impatient lives

Straining toward the future
Believing we are advancing

*xanas: water nymphs found in Celtic lore

White Dove

Paloma blanca
Heavenly spirit
Crossing the Bravo
Music of the pueblo
Jose Alfredo

Picasso and Spain
Art and war
Cordoba Toledo
White dove
Dark tears

Andalucía
Fire and ice
Sierra Nevada
Silver-throated
Antonio Molina

White dove
Golden beak
Silver wings
Sentiments fly
Feelings flow

Hear the song
Come to the river
Bathe with me
White dove
Of the spirit

The Mosaic of Spain

—De Madrid al cielo.

When Philip traveled in the south of Spain with Maruja, he realized that his trip had begun years earlier in Chicago, his city of raw power and values that had given him the strength to persist in building a meaningful life.

Then came the U.S. Army and the Cold War. Japan. Cuba. The intelligence services and the testing of his values.

Next was Mexico with its humanism and warmth. There he found a magnificent wife and the thread of love she gave him to understand trauma and erase it. Tom Berkley guided him to a balanced life. Along the way, Philip watched people around him give up their values, flounder, and fall into confusion, unhappiness, and even death.

Chicago had sustained him. Mexico rewarded him. And now Spain became a shining reality. It was multicultural, full of character, geography, and history, and it opened to Europe. Earlier trips to Spain had been to the north: Basque Bilbao, Picasso's Guernica, and the Guggenheim of Frank Gehrey. During these trips Philip studied Spain's early history. The Celtic flow from the Danube in Hungary into Asturias and Galicia, led from La Coruña by Brogan into Ireland. He read of the Scandinavians traveling from their Eskiltuna to the Eskalduna of the Basques and to the Esk River in Scotland. The Viking longboats sliced down the rivers of northern Spain, around the southern coast, and into the Mediterranean. La Dama de Elche.

This time the trip was to the south to reach the warm heart and sentiment of Andalusia. Philip and Maruja traveled from Madrid by the high-speed Ave train to Sevilla, where they stayed in the Casas de la Juderia and walked the Barrio of the Holy Cross. They crossed the Arab Guadalquivir River to reach Triana, its reflection shimmering in the quiet waters. Triana was home to flamenco, the gypsy Christ El Cachorro, and the Virgin of Hope, patroness of bullfighters. They recrossed the Guadalquivir and lunched near the tobacco factory of Bizet's *Carmen*. They entered the enormous central cathedral with its Moorish tower and studied the four giant metal figures carrying the catafalque with the remains of Columbus, who departed from nearby

Palos to cross the Atlantic and find his New World. The voyages of Columbus made Sevilla the richest city in Spain until 1717, when the Spanish government transferred its New World commercial center to the southern port of Cadiz. Cadiz was the next stop on their trip. Maruja's mother's family was from Cadiz.

Cadiz

Their trip to the port of Cadiz, located seventy miles south of Sevilla, was intended to reach the origins of Maruja's family. They were from Cadiz three generations earlier via Manuela Jurado, an Andalusian beauty worthy of a painting by Julio Romero of Cordoba. Manuela Jurado left Cadiz with a Basque ship captain to live in Mexico. The details of her life in Spain were lost in the mists of the past. The truth was that Maruja inherited her beauty and her memories passed across generations.

Known originally as Gades, Cadiz is a three thousand-year-old port founded mythically by the Greek demigod Hercules though actually by the Phoenicians. It is known as a cup of sparkling silver on the Costa de Luz, warmed by breezes from nearby Africa. In Cadiz, Philip and Maruja stayed at a hotel facing the sea. Directly below them along the shore walk there was a statue of Gades, the mythical goddess who gave the city its name. They visited the statue and walked to nearby seafood restaurants where they ate fresh clams, shrimp, and lobster and drank Spanish wines. They went by car into the old part of the city and roamed its narrow, wandering streets and browsed its shops. But Maruja always returned to the statue of Gades by the sea. She and the statue shared a common tie with the mythical past.

On Sunday Philip accompanied Maruja to a service at the Church of Santo Tomas. It was five blocks from their hotel. The only Saint Thomas Philip really knew was Thomas Lucius Berkley of Oakland, his African American older brother who had guided his life. The church was filled with a large number of young people who participated actively in the service. Their enthusiasm contrasted with the aimless secularism that Philip had noted in Madrid and in much of modern Spain.

There was a moment in the service when people turned to one another to offer a wish for peace. Philip had noticed a young, black-haired, black-eyed, statuesque Gaetana woman in the row directly in front of him. When she turned and saw Maruja, she smiled and winked and gave her the warm family greeting of a sister. It was an epiphany of beauty and understanding between the two look-alike Gaetanas. Philip asked Maruja what she had said to the woman to produce such a moment. Maruja replied that she had not said a word.

Then the young priest at the lectern spoke. Philip learned later that he was a secular Spanish priest raised in Africa. Instead of making traditional statements about the past, he concentrated his message entirely on the present. He quoted the empty promises made by rich countries to reduce poverty in Africa. He spoke of Africa's need for eighteen million teachers and how countries there paid four times in foreign debt what they spent on education and health.

The priest criticized excessive consumerism in rich countries and lives based on brands and material goods. He urged people to practice simplicity, share what they had, and sensitize their hearts to the suffering of the poor. Global warming and the environment would eventually limit the production of goods, and people would have to do with less. He argued it was better to start understanding and practicing now what was coming inevitably.

Philip left the church awakened by the clarity and directness of the message he had heard. Cadiz would become a turning point in his search for meaning in Spain. He had been focused on the past and planned to travel with Maruja to Ronda, where he could walk in the central Plaza Mondragon, and then to Granada, where he could research and rekindle the past of the Arabs, Jews, and Christians who had lived there in tolerance for a time. But the secular priest brought him abruptly into the present. Reality eclipsed romanticism. Kristin Lavrensdatter had understood. One cannot live in the present by hiding in a cloistered past.

Philip thought back to Mexico, where he had chosen to work in programs for the poor while many people around him were busy accumulating money. Some of these people were now facing discomfort and pressure in an overpopulated country further stressed by rising dissatisfaction among the militant poor. They and their children were not sure of what to do. Philip decided to stop writing about the past. He would write ideas that might help a virtual generation live inside reality.

Twelve Lights

Philip had enjoyed the beauty and history of Spain and its rich multiculture, people, music, and wines. Then the secular priest in Cadiz jarred him into the hard realities of the present. He realized that people need lights to find their way during the transitions of the emerging world. He would write more about this later, but he began by identifying twelve lights that life had given him in the hope that they might help others.

- Recognize that life today is confusing. We are making blind choices in a virtual world, often with unhappy results. There is a better way.

- The answer to each problem is inside you. The way out is in. If you do not solve inside first, then you will not solve your outside problems.

- Drop all resentments. They blind you and force you to live in a past that is unchangeable.

- They do not let you live in the present. The present is now. Not yesterday.

- Drop your pride and ego—the belief that yours is the only way. Practice humility and an open mind. Humility opens the doors to wisdom.

- Stop looking for perfection in others and in yourself and feeling disappointed or guilty when you do not find it. Understand that everyone is imperfect. It is the human condition. Allow everyone, including yourself, a large margin for error. Pardon and move on.

- Do things. Participate. Every day take one step beyond what you did yesterday.

- If something is impossible do it anyway. Make mistakes. Learn. Doing is the key, not talking about doing.

- Try again and again. Never stop at any time or age. Persist. Doing will become a habit.

- Forget yourself as often as you can. Find ways to help others reach their goals. As you do this you will surprisingly reach your own goals.

- Simplify the complexity around you. Whenever possible reduce your choices to three. Then reflect and make your final choice.

- Base each choice on being yourself, not someone else. Gradually you will find out who you really are. Finding out brings happy surprises.

- Understand by going beyond logic. Pay attention to your inner feelings because they give you moments of clarity when the truth finally reaches you.

- Time ripens understanding. Give yourself a little more time to find answers to your questions. Reflect, decide, and do. Learn and move on. Always move on.

Find Me

God says
I am love
I am the way
Find me

I am within
The quantum interior
And outside
Everywhere

In the experience
Of everyday life
In a moment
Beyond words

In illusion and reality
When the ego dies
And humility opens
The door to wisdom

Search for me
I am there
Inside the heart
Find me

Meditation

Love

God is love
Put God first
And everything else
Falls into place
Love all people
And cultures and races
Love the poor and children
And your enemies
Love through thoughts
And words and acts
Love understands
Love forgives
Love heals

Acts

God of love
Through acts let me serve
My family and the community
Use the talents you have given me
And fulfill the potential of my nature
Bring the spirit of Christ
To earthly realities
Endure hardships
And carry your cross
With humility and patience
Give love
And honor you

Humility

God of love I seek humility
In order to understand your mandates
When I am silent and patient
When I listen and seek to learn
And do not judge
When I am humble with everyone
My pride leaves me
And your wisdom appears
I welcome humility
As the door to wisdom

Gratitude

God of love I thank you for suffering
And the peace you give me
When I understand
The opportunity I have within it
And I act
I thank you for suffering
And for your love and wisdom
And for humility
For each opportunity
To serve others
And carry your cross

Wisdom

God is the giver of wisdom
Through meditation and prayer
God give me wisdom
I seek to learn
Wisdom understands
And guides and teaches
Justice and firmness
Balance and moderation
Awareness of your true good
Wisdom makes everything new
Shows you what is within your grasp
Learn wisdom and good things
Come to you

The Valley

The heart and life
Seek warmth and light
In some distant heaven
While on earth
A gentle breeze and water
Whisper in a valley of silence
Beyond the wail
Of human grief
Rising from the soul

Far away an engine drones
In dull metallic tones
Nearby a butterfly
And a warbling bird
Give proof of life
And the flow of energy
Indestructible and eternal
In changing forms
And the God of love within

Journey

How long we searched
For truth and perfection
In ignorance and fear
In mirrors and reflection

In suns and stars
Statues and stones
Totems and trees
Animals and bones

In wind and water
Energy and light
Fire and earth
Money and might

In the virtual world
Where we now reside
In finite space
With nowhere to hide

Forced at last
To look within
To find the place where
God has always been

In the world beyond words
The fourth chakra apart
Compassion for others
Gaia and the heart

The Gift

They canceled my meeting
And gave me the hour
In Frondoso Valley
With its mystical power

I walked with Maruja
Her limitless love
The breath of God
In the trees above

Sunlight and shadow
Stones and stream
I saw reality
Inside the dream

Red bougainvillea
Flowers of gold
Clusters of beauty
My heart will hold

Now and always
We are one
Our walk together
Is never done

Necklace

Pearls pink and gray and white
Luminescent in the fading light
Of that autumn evening
When you walked with her

She gave you her love
Every day without condition
The years were moments
They passed and now

She tires and smiles
You care for her
And understand what is coming
And you thank your God of love

For each brief moment
Echoing in the eternal present
Pearls pink and gray and white
Luminescent in the fading light

Wonder

Light from a fiery sun
In a spiraling galaxy
Reaches a single raindrop
Balanced on a blade
Of bright green grass
And it glistens and becomes
A crystal of exquisite art

I watch and wonder
Who did I touch
Who did I help
With well-intentioned acts
And a few words distilled
From the crucible of my life
Now approaching infinity

Emerging Beauty

I searched relentlessly for love
    and could not find it in others
I strove to reach their standards
    and fell short again and again
My glaring imperfections
    were clear to all and duly noted
I suffered inside and outside
    I saw how other people suffered
I felt their pain and I decided
    that if I could not conquer my own pain
I would help them conquer theirs
Day by day I gave years of quiet service
    and saw a few improve their lives
I repeated and repeated my imperfect attempts
    and when I returned home to reach others
I found that I had reached myself
And I saw in everyone
    the emerging beauty of fractal imperfection
And I understood that by rolling the Sisyphus stone
    day after day after day I had found myself
I am grateful ever so grateful for each day and lesson
    in this unending trip

Epilogue

He was old now, and at the wedding of his first granddaughter, Maricarmen, he sat at a center table on the colonial-style patio of the building in the Centro Historico in downtown Mexico City, flanked by the people he had journeyed with. On his right was his wife Maruja, who had given him love and loyalty every day of their life together. To his left was Velda, who had come from Oakland to enjoy the wedding and to see in the granddaughter the accumulated effects of what Philip, Maruja, she, and Tom had built together. Philip had to look across the generations if he wanted to understand the contradictions of life. This was his opportunity.

Philip saw everyone and everything, and he used the perspective that had arrived in him with age to put the pieces together. He saw in Maricarmen the thoughtfulness and inner peace of his mother. Her new husband, a clear-thinking engineer, well educated in the graces of life, reflected in his face the deep love he had for his new wife.

Maruja, driven always by maternal love, radiated happiness and energy. She had seen long ago the qualities and potential in the young couple.

Tom was no longer with them. He had suffered and led and taught, and his presence shone in Velda, in Philip and Maruja and their children, and now in the next generation. His warmth was present, as was his good humor and the quality he had maintained during the fight for fairness in spite of his many hurts. His dreams were there too, and above all was his wisdom.

Philip reflected quietly. At one point during the evening he suddenly and finally saw meaning in everything past and present. His mother had been abandoned by her husband, and yet she had sent her son to Mexico to get to know him and to find a better life. He had found it not in money or social position but in the love and quality of his wife, in the wisdom of Tom and Velda, in his children, and now in their children. He realized that he could not understand his own life until he went beyond it. And when he went beyond and put the pieces together, then life had depth and meaning and reward.

He had made his outward journey from Depression-times Chicago on the three rivers of his life: the Mississippi, the Bravo, and the

Guadalquivir. His inward trip had taken him from blindness to seeing to feeling and understanding. And the values of his home had never left him. His mother had been denied the right to come to Mexico, and now she was present at the first wedding of the next generation.

Philip had built on her values and the love of Maruja and the wisdom of Tom and Velda, and it had brought him to this evening of extreme beauty. He focused on the now-points of the hundreds of candles flickering on all sides of the colonial balcony that overlooked the patio, which was filled with hundreds of people. He saw his now-point in the quantum space, and he understood that it was real. He thought of Alcalá and Toledo and the knight of the sad countenance. At the end of his life he had become a man of clear judgment who finally saw things as they were with calm and serenity. The knight's epitaph said that he had battled in a material world that he found less important than his dreams and beliefs. He had lived as a fool, but through the experience and clarity of age he had died a sage.

Printed in the United States
217295BV00001B/337-360/P

9 780595 530519